The Rul

St. Benedict

VINTAGE SPIRITUAL CLASSICS

General Editors
John F. Thornton
Susan B. Varenne

ALSO AVAILABLE

The Desert Fathers
The Imitation of Christ
The Little Flowers of St. Francis of Assisi

The Rule *of* St. Benedict

IN ENGLISH

EDITOR

Timothy Fry, O.S.B.

ASSOCIATE EDITORS

Imogene Baker, O.S.B.

Timothy Horner, O.S.B.

Augusta Raabe, O.S.B.

Mark Sheridan, O.S.B.

VINTAGE SPIRITUAL CLASSICS

VINTAGE BOOKS
A DIVISION OF RANDOM HOUSE, INC.
NEW YORK

A VINTAGE SPIRITUAL CLASSICS ORIGINAL, MAY 1998
FIRST EDITION

Copyright © 1981 by the Order of St. Benedict, Inc., Collegeville, Minnesota
About the Vintage Spiritual Classics, Preface to the Vintage Spiritual Classics Edition,
and Chronology of Christian Monasticism, 150 B.C.—600 A.D. Copyright © 1998
by Random House, Inc.

Library of Congress Cataloging-in-Publication Data
Benedict, Saint, Abbot of Monte Cassino.
The rule of St. Benedict in English / editor, Timothy Fry :
associate editors, Imogene Baker . . . [et al.] 1st ed.
p. cm. — (Vintage spiritual classics)
Includes bibliographical references.
ISBN 0-375-70017-X
1. Benedictines—Rules   I. Fry, Timothy, 1915– . II. Title.
III. Series.
BX3004.A2   1998
255'.106—dc21   97-46359
CIP

www.randomhouse.com

Book design by Fritz Metsch

Printed in the United States of America
20 19 18 17 16 15 14 13

A NOTE ON THE TEXT

For the scriptural passages in this translation, the Vulgate numbering of chapters is followed; for the psalms, the Hebrew numbers are also given. Direct quotations from Scripture are italicized. The Latin text from which this translation was made is that of J. Neufville in A. De Vogüé, *La Règle de saint Benoît,* Sources Chrétiennes 181–182 (Paris: Les Éditions du Cerf, 1972). The translation is taken from the unabridged edition of *RB 1980: The Rule of St. Benedict in Latin and English with Notes,* ed. Timothy Fry, O.S.B. (Collegeville, Minn.: The Liturgical Press, 1981). Readers may refer to this unabridged edition for an account of the monks and nuns involved in the work of translation and for information on monastic subjects.

CONTENTS

ABOUT THE
VINTAGE SPIRITUAL CLASSICS

by John F. Thornton and Susan B. Varenne, General Editors

A turn or shift of sorts is becoming evident in the reflections of men and women today on their life experiences. Not quite as adamantly secular and, perhaps, a little less insistent on material satisfactions, the reading public has recently developed a certain attraction to testimonies that human life is leavened by a Presence that blesses and sanctifies. Recovery, whether from addictions or personal traumas, illness, or even painful misalignments in human affairs, is evolving from the standard therapeutic goal of enhanced self-esteem. Many now seek a deeper healing that embraces the whole person, including the soul. Contemporary books provide accounts of the invisible assistance of angels. The laying on of hands in prayer has made an appearance at the hospital bedside. Guides for the spiritually perplexed have risen to the top of best-seller lists. The darkest shadows of skepticism and unbelief, which have eclipsed the presence of the Divine in our rational age, are beginning to lighten and part.

If the power and presence of God are real and effective, what do they mean for human experience? What does He offer to men and women, and what does He ask in return? How do we recognize Him? Know Him? Respond to Him? God has a reputation for being both benevolent and wrathful. Which will He be for me and when? Can these aspects of the Divine somehow be reconciled? Where is God when I suffer? Can I lose Him? Is God truthful, and are His promises to be trusted?

Are we really as precious to God as we are to ourselves and our loved ones? Do His providence and amazing grace guide our faltering steps toward Him, even in spite of ourselves? Will God abandon us if the sin is serious enough, or if we have episodes of resistance and forgetfulness? These are fundamental questions any person might address to God during a lifetime. They are pressing and difficult, often becoming wounds in the soul of the person who yearns for the power and courage of hope, especially in stressful times.

The Vintage Spiritual Classics present the testimony of writers across the centuries who have considered all these difficulties and who have pondered the mysterious ways, unfathomable mercies, and deep consolations afforded by God to those who call upon Him from out of the depths of their lives. These writers, then, are our companions, even our champions, in a common effort to discern the meaning of God in personal experience. For God is personal to us. To whom does He speak if not to us, provided we have the desire to hear Him deep within our hearts?

Each volume opens with a specially commissioned essay by a well-known contemporary writer that offers the reader an appreciation of its intrinsic value. A chronology of the general historical context of each work is provided, as are suggestions for further reading.

We offer a final word about the act of reading these spiritual classics. From the very earliest accounts of monastic practice—dating back to the fourth century—it is evident that a form of reading called *lectio divina* ("divine" or "spiritual reading") was essential to any deliberate spiritual life. This kind of reading is quite different from that of scanning a text for useful facts and bits of information, or advancing along an exciting plot line to a climax in the action. It is, rather, a meditative approach, by which the reader seeks to taste and savor the beauty and truth of every phrase and passage. This process of contemplative reading has the effect of enkindling in the reader compunction for past behavior that has been less than beautiful and true. At the same time, it increases the desire to seek a realm where all that is lovely and unspoiled may be found. There are four steps in *lectio divina*: first, to read, next to meditate, then to rest in the sense of God's nearness, and, ultimately, to resolve to govern one's actions in the light of new understanding. This kind of reading is itself an act of prayer. And, indeed, it is in prayer that God manifests His Presence to us.

by Thomas Moore

Fifteen hundred years ago, a young man studying in Rome became disgusted with the paganism he saw there and decided to live in solitude in a cave some distance outside the city. In that decision Benedict enacted a fantasy that has inflamed the hearts of men and women before and since—the idea of making a life apart from the crowd, in a style at odds with the norm.

Not everyone so inspired retreats to an actual cave or enters monastic life, and yet anyone, even today, might catch the spirit and look for solitude in a home by the sea or in a hike deep into the woods or in a style of living contrary in most respects to current standards. As I read *The Rule of St. Benedict,* I'm interested in the interpretations and historical observations of scholars and monks, but I'm more fascinated by the imagination behind *The Rule*—not the thoughts of a single person, Benedict, but the possibility of envisioning life as profoundly contemplative and thoroughly communal.

The Rule

Part one of the monk's fantasy is the decision not to live as everyone else does. The man or woman looks around and sees a way of life that is chaotic, irreverent, or unethical and decides to design a life according to different standards. Part two is sketching out the new way in a rule. Most, of course, do not go so far as to make a literal rule or even to choose one, but subtly and originally they might think up ways of doing things that will be unique and full of value. Every thoughtful person, no matter what his or her lifestyle may be, has a rule, one archetype of which might be *The Rule of St. Benedict.*

In our day of existential self-discovery, individualism, and the literalization of freedom, it may seem odd to reflect on one's culture, decide to live an examined and thoughtful life, and then choose a strict rule of conduct and attitude. *The Rule of St. Benedict* is full of sentiments and statements bound to offend modern sensibilities—corporal punishment, ownership in common, humility, proscriptions against laughter, submission of the will in obedience. Doesn't this turn toward humility, obedience, and the frugal life look like compensation for a challenging world or escape from responsibility by giving one's will to an abbot?

In spite of its claim to require "nothing harsh, nothing burdensome," *The Rule* seems quite tough, and indeed the very idea of following a rule seems to create a way of life dangerously subservient and masochistic. The very word "rule" is connected to many terms that appear contrary to freedom: regulation, ruler (both leader and straight edge), king *(rex),* correct, rectangle, rectitude, and rectum. At first glance, following a rule doesn't appear to be a desirable alternative to a materialistic world.

But *regula,* Latin for rule, even in the time of the ancient Romans, also referred to a pattern or a model. The very straight-edged rule that keeps things in line can also help design a house. From the creative point of view, the monastic rule is an instrument for shaping a particular kind of life for which a person has deep and genuine desire. It's a tough life in certain ways—the rule can be harsh—but it is also in its own way liberating. It frees a person from the unspoken rules of the society at large and offers an alternative.

For many years, I lived under a monastic rule—*The Rule of Saint Augustine,* not Benedict's—and I found the regulations both difficult and liberating. There is no doubt that a monastic rule can stir up masochistic responses in some people, so that they feel constantly under the eye of the superior or unable to be themselves and let their spirits shine. The rule can give rise to anger, resentment, and depression. In my experience, however, people living under the monastic rule generally have a good sense of humor and a lusty love of life. Sadistic authorities and masochistic subordinates appear here and there, but they are a minority.

Monks soften the harshness of the rule by subjecting ancient regulations to constant interpretation and reflection. Just as civil laws can be interpreted strictly or in a relaxed fashion, so the monastic rule is open to fresh consideration and readings. Here again we can see the rule as a pattern or model instead of a literal list of dos and don'ts. It is the embodiment of a vision and a philosophy that is perhaps better lived in the spirit of its origins than as a legal document.

Men and women attracted to the ancient *Rule of St. Benedict* are not drawn, I'm sure, by any invitation to subject themselves to rigid authoritarianism. *The Rule* gives flesh to a vision in which certain values are given higher status than they would have in ordinary society. Specifically, the monk turns to *The Rule of St. Benedict* to find the outlines of a life dedicated to community and contemplation.

Community

Modern culture is dedicated to the freedom and fulfillment of the individual. We are caught up in intricate social structures, and we continue to invent new technological ways of communicating with each other, and yet the person drawn to monastic life realizes that a busy, involved society doesn't make a community. A family is usually a community; so, often, is a neighborhood. But society in a larger sense doesn't share the values of deep altruism and self-denial one finds detailed in *The Rule*. Nor is there in society that special kind of mutual love, sometimes called *agape,* that characterizes a true community.

The Rule of St. Benedict doesn't address community love explicitly, but it does set up the conditions under which it can flourish. Common ownership of property, for example, can provide a deep grounding for community life, and, in fact, it's difficult to imagine the radical commonality of monasticism without it. This is a fundamental way, of course, in which the monk differs from the ordinary person, for whom the acquisition of property gives life meaning.

As a monk, I never found the lack of possessions a big problem. Once in a while it got in the way, as when I might want to buy a certain book or recording or to undertake a certain trip, but notice the sentiment there—"I want." Common ownership fosters an attitude that moves away from passing personal desires, while preserving the deeper, grander wish to live a life in tune with one's values and philosophy. Besides, monks usually have everything they need without the anxiety of personal responsibility for making money and paying bills.

Worship in common also fosters the spirit of community. When people meditate, pray, and chant together, they evoke a sense of community that, though highly spiritual, helps them connect with each other in invisible, mysterious, and inexplicable ways. In ordinary life, people may try to forge a community spirit by gathering together and doing all the "community" things that are supposed to work—common projects, pot-luck dinners, and heart-to-heart conversations.

In the monastic life, intense communal living takes place in an atmosphere of silence. Monks don't talk a great deal, nor, as *The Rule* abjures more than once, do they laugh and joke foolishly. The accent here is on *foolishly*. Monks live a serious life of dedication. The ordinary modern person seems not to think much about a philosophy of life, and one wonders sometimes how serious we are about life. We may have certain moral slogans and we may be loyal to a political party, but if newspapers, magazines, and other media are any indication, as a society we are not terribly interested in philosophy, theology, or even political ideas. We have reduced politics to personalities and contests and don't seem to take seriously the philosophies that lie just beneath the surface of our practical decisions.

Benedict also asks for a way of speaking that would enhance community. "Your way of acting should be different from the world's way," he says, emphasizing the point that the whole idea of *The Rule* is to create an alternative way of life. "Never give a hollow greeting of peace or turn away when someone needs your love. . . . Speak the truth with heart and tongue." Here we have three radical suggestions that clearly could transform social and political discourse. If we never spoke hollow words of affection to each other, never turned away when someone needed an expression of our love, and spoke from the heart, we would automatically be making a different world, and we would find ourselves in the thick of real community.

We don't have to take these suggestions as idealistic or perfectionistic. By living regularly (another "rule" word) from a deep place, by speaking for what we know is in our hearts, and by responding to the needs we see around us, we would find ourselves in a real family, a true neighborhood, and possibly in a city or town with a genuine community spirit. To live with this degree of authenticity and transparency requires reflection. We would have to avoid the typical unconsciousness we feel in hollow everyday speech and in our neglect of those around us. It also may entail a certain unavoidable naïveté, because the monk lives outside the perimeters of worldly wisdom.

Obedience

The Rule has a lot to say about obedience and authority. It makes three points that are essential lest we get a superficial or literal idea about obedience: (1) The abbot speaks for Christ. His authority is not personal, and he is obeyed not as a person is obeyed, but as the representative of a far deeper and more subtle authority. (2) The abbot's concern is care of the soul—Benedict's phrase. Social organization and smooth running of the operation of the monastery are not the goals of this kind of obedience. It is possible to listen to the voice, the interpretations, and even the will of another and hear a message from a mysterious and profound place. The challenge for the abbot is to exercise authority in such a way that it is not personal and not political in the usual sense but does in fact bear the imprint of a spiritual message. (3) Finally, Benedict recommends mutual obedience.

Ever since a priest once reminded me that the word "obedience" literally means *to hear,* I have been intrigued by the idea of friends and family members obeying each other. We tend to hear the word "obedience" with overtones of literal dominance and subjection, but, less literally, it is possible to hear deeper voices and deeper words in the sentences that come out of the mouths of friends. There we may find guidance, not by taking their authority personally but by realizing that another person may intuit or perceive things about ourselves of which we are ignorant. With care, caution, and some interpretation, we may find the direction our lives require in the passing words of our friends. Sometimes the very sound of these words may signal greater import as they resound with unusual force and meaning.

Humility

In many ways, monasticism turns life upside down, inverting values that seem to the world to be prudent and natural. In the world, we're told to succeed, enjoy prestige, stand out as an individual, and be confident and strong. Modern psychology, in particular, favors independence over dependence, confidence over feelings of inferiority, avoidance of pain, and a strong will. *The Rule* says just the opposite: submit to authority, feel your inferiority, embrace suffering, and have no will of your own. How can anyone live this rule and enjoy emotional health?

The Rule makes it clear that familiar modern values come from a purely secular frame of mind. As Rudolf Otto says in his classic definition, religion is fundamentally a sense of awe. It is based on an awareness that we are indeed quite small in the scope of things. If we want to live a less secular life, one that includes religious virtues, as well as secular prudence, then we may have to discover the implications of this existential humility.

Benedict lists twelve ways of being humble, beginning, interestingly, with the fear of God—living a life with eternal as well as temporal implications—and, along with this injunction, without lust. One of the many things monks have perceived for centuries is the necessity, in a life based on care of the soul, for sexual containment. Some may interpret celibacy and purity literally and disown them as impractical. But if we consider the monastic view of sex carefully, we may find that it's possible to redefine sexuality or to sublimate sexual desire in ways that are neither repressive nor unhealthy. This task, too vast to spell out in a few words, would involve taking monastic celibacy and common love seriously and bringing them into dialogue with our ideas about a fertile and satisfying sex life. The result would be an intensification of sexuality and a fresh appreciation for limits on sensual desire.

Benedict also suggests many ways for feeling our existential inferiority. This is different from pathological emotions related to confusion over power and self-worth. In the context of the universe and all of nature, we are in fact quite inferior. We make mistakes, misspeak and misjudge, fail, fall down, and fall apart. If we habitually disown this natural inferiority of the soul, then we will be condemned to bounce back and forth between pride and self-effacement. It makes psychological sense to affirm our inferiority, thus grounding our confidence in an accurate view of ourselves. Inferiority is only part of the picture, but to deny it is to set ourselves up for a lifetime of trying not to make mistakes and denying our faults.

In fact, Benedict recommends confessing to our failures and acknowledging our insignificance. In literature that bears a similar appreciation for humankind's insignificance, such as the biblical Book of Job or the works of Samuel Beckett or certain of Emily Dickinson's poems, I find a dark strain of humor. I suspect that the monk's life is funny in a similar way. The humility Benedict requires is genuine, and yet those monasteries in which humility is truly lived are places full of humor and vitality, while those that give only lip service to humility can be dour places made rigid with their pride. Benedict's humility, on the surface so contrary to modern hygienic values, resurrects a comic sense of life.

Contemplation

The emphasis in *The Rule* on contemplative practices gives it its exceptional value and, of course, over the centuries has inspired many reformers, organizations, and individuals to create fresh ways of being contemplative. *The Rule* refers to the chanting of psalms as the *Opus Dei,* or Work of God, and for the monk it is certainly true that common prayer, carried out in a spirit of contemplation and with beauty, is his or her central work. The followers of Benedict's *Rule* have become leaders in the areas of liturgical music, ritual, and sacred art, the importance of which seems not clear to people at large. Yet this focus is more directly aimed at caring for the soul than are the pursuit of theology and philosophy or the development of social activities.

Benedict's attention to reading adds another dimension to the contemplative life. In modern life we read mainly for information or entertainment, and writing about books tends to be critical rather than appreciative and exploratory. We have yet to rediscover the monastic practice of contemplative reading which is carried out with care, attention to beauty and form, and a meditative attitude.

The combination of being aware of the divine presence everywhere, chanting the Divine Office with special care to its art, praying briefly but devotionally, reading contemplatively, and treating manual labor for the community as a part of spiritual practice—all these five daily give life a special quality, a tranquility and calm that are difficult or impossible to find in the non-monastic world. It seems true that ours is still an age of anxiety, not a psychological problem but an existential condition created by the busy, productive, and unthoughtful style of modern work, play, and home life.

The monastic rule addresses this fundamental problem with simple but effective means that together relieve this anxiety. Monks often refer to "the world" as a place distinct from the monastery, and it is true that the monastic style, inspired by the basic rule, creates a structure for living that is in many ways different from that of the world at large. The music, reading, prayer, and common life create an alternative culture in which the soul is the center of attention.

The Monastic Spirit in the Modern World

Though ancient and, if taken literally, somewhat out of date, *The Rule of St. Benedict* is as fresh and relevant today as it ever was. The anxiety of worldly life has certainly increased, and today people admit that they need a way out of the tempo and busyness of life. As an actual life structure, monasticism is not as popular as it once was, perhaps, but it has as much importance as ever. The mere presence of a monastery inspires the rest of the world, for it remembers, keeps us all mindful, of alternative ways of living that are more contemplative than active. Even today, lay people attach themselves to monasteries to keep that special spirit alive in themselves. Another way to seed ordinary life with the monastic spirit might be to read this rule not for its historical importance or as a literal guide for monks, but to inspire anyone in the direction of contemplation. In the midst of our busy lives we can practice the spirit of this rule.

In our families and cities we are members of a community, and there we could deepen our sense of ownership by taking more responsibility for the things and activities in our common life. The monastic spirit could transform our understanding of politics, for example. We could pray with reasonable attention and with beauty and care, and we could read contemplatively and generally comport ourselves more thoughtfully. We could cultivate silence and beauty in all aspects of our lives, from home to work to public places. We could commit ourselves to stability and faithfulness in our homes and towns as a way of countering the modern tendency to be distant, unattached, and inconstant. We could live more simply and humbly without losing any of our sophistication. With nothing harsh or burdensome, we would all let this rule give ordinary life a dimension of common service and emotional tranquility that it usually lacks.

The monk is not an anachronism, nor is *The Rule of St. Benedict* antique and irrelevant. It is modern life, rather, that is not in accord with the fundamental needs of the human heart. From the viewpoint of the human soul, our modern style of living is the irrelevancy. By not enjoying a genuine common life and by not giving ourselves a degree of contemplation, we wound our need for emotional quiet and for meaning. And so it is appropriate to return to this ancient sketch of an alternative life, to reread it and discuss it, and, with imagination and reflection, bring its spirit into the workplace, the home, and the city, where it could transform a culture of anxiety into a community of peace and mutual regard.

INTRODUCTION

by Timothy Fry

Pope John Paul II addressed two documents in 1981 to the entire Catholic Church and to "all men and women of good will." Inspired by a most urgent desire to help people improve their basic human relations, he wrote the encyclical "On Human Work" and the apostolic exhortation "The Role of the Family in Modern Society." St. Benedict's times were as turbulent as our own, though for very different reasons. He wrote his Rule primarily for monks, but its sound principles for working together and living together have proved relevant to people of all classes of society through fifteen hundred years.

Benedict (c. 480–547) lived in Italy when the great Roman Empire was disintegrating. Rome had fallen to the barbarians in 410 and was sacked again in 455. Romulus Augustulus, the last emperor, was deposed in 476. Theodoric of the Ostrogoths maintained peace during a long reign (493–526), but upon his death the Eastern emperor Justinian tried to regain Rome, and through the remaining years of the century there was constant war as other barbarian tribes invaded the Italian peninsula.

Sometime during the reign of Theodoric, Benedict as a young man left his native Nursia in Umbria to attend school in Rome, but became disgusted with the paganism he saw and renounced the world to live in solitude in a cave at Subiaco, some thirty miles east of Rome. Evidently he had undergone a deep religious experience. In time he came to the notice of people in the neighborhood, and some monks asked him to be their abbot. He consented with reluctance, and after some time the recalcitrant monks sought to poison him. Later another group of monks joined him, and he established twelve monasteries of twelve monks each.

Experience with the envy of the local clergy led Benedict to abandon this settlement, and with some disciples he founded a monastery on the mountain above Cassino, about eighty miles south of Rome. His fame as a holy person spread throughout the area; even the king of the Goths, Totila, came to see him. About the year 547 he died. Pope St. Gregory the Great (590–604), whose second book of *The Dialogues* is the only source for information on St. Benedict, notes that St. Scholastica was his sister (traditionally known as his twin sister).

Apart from these meager facts, nothing more is known of the life of St. Benedict. But most of the information from St. Gregory can be corroborated by other historical events of the time. Gregory did not set out to write a biography; his purpose was to show that there were holy people in Italy, not just in the East, and that St. Benedict was a great miracle worker. He mentions the Rule of St. Benedict and commends it for its discretion and lucidity of style. "If anyone wishes to know his character and life more precisely, he may find in the ordinances of that Rule a complete account of the abbot's practice; for the holy man cannot have taught otherwise than as he lived."

Writers after St. Gregory have noted the same discretion in St. Benedict's Rule, and this quality more than any other accounts in great part for its longevity. The fact that many men and women throughout the world live it today is supporting evidence.

In the unsettled, strife-torn Italy of the sixth century, Benedict's Rule offered definitive direction and established an ordered way of life that gave security and stability. He sought to lay down "nothing harsh, nothing burdensome," but was intent on encouraging the person coming to the monastery: "Do not be daunted immediately by fear and run away from the road that leads to salvation."

Benedict calls his Rule "a little rule for beginners." It contains directions for all aspects of the monastic life, from establishing the abbot as superior, the arrangement of psalms for prayers, measures for correction of faults, to details of clothing and the amount of food and drink. The reader will note that some customs are outmoded today, and monks have accordingly modified some of these.

St. Benedict taught that if the monk seeks to answer the call of God—"If you hear his voice today, do not harden your heart"—then he must put all else aside and follow the teaching of Christ in obedience. To this end St. Benedict established a "school for the Lord's service," a place where monks learn to serve the Lord in obedience to their abbot, who "is believed to hold the place of Christ." His spirituality is Christocentric: "the love of Christ must come before all else." After a year of trial, the novice promises stability, fidelity to monastic life, and obedience. St. Benedict expected his monks to advance on the "path of God's commandments, [their] hearts overflowing with the inexpressible delight of love."

Benedict was a keen observer of human nature and realized that people often fail (the abbot must "distrust his own frailty"). He was concerned to help the weak, and consequently he enjoined that the abbot "so regulate and arrange all matters that souls may be saved and the brothers may go about their activities without justifiable grumbling." Benedict looked to the heart; he sought a spirit of willingness ("First and foremost, there must be no word or sign of the evil of grumbling, no manifestation of it for any reason at all") and sincerity ("Never give a hollow greeting of peace"; "Let us stand to sing the psalms in such a way that our minds are in harmony with our voices").

The so-called penal code (chs. 23–30, 43–46) is more accurately seen as correctional measures designed for the reformation and healing of the person, not a rigid, brutal structure imposed legalistically. St. Benedict stressed the importance of the person and the relationship of persons living together. He respected the freedom of the person (the novice is free to leave at any time; the monk who leaves may be received back even a third time). If there is strictness, the purpose is to "amend faults and safeguard love." He directed the abbot to "arrange everything that the strong have something to yearn for and the weak nothing to run from." It is a humane approach to personal relationships. But it is an approach based on the supernatural: "that in all things God may be glorified." Benedict was a God-oriented man leading like-minded people on the way of the Gospel. In St. Gregory's words, he was a man of God *(vir Dei)*.

St. Benedict's Abbey
Atchison, Kansas

Feast of St. Benedict
21 March 1982

CHRONOLOGY OF CHRISTIAN MONASTICISM
150 B.C. – 600 A.D.

Pre-Christian Monasticism

150 B.C.–68 A.D. The Essenes/Qumranites were a pre-Christian religious sect of Jewish Palestinians who lived ascetic lives in small communities on the western shore of the Dead Sea. They practiced fervent, rigorous observance of the Torah in expectation of a Davidic/Aaronic Messiah. In 68 A.D., these cells, or communities, were destroyed by the Romans. The Dead Sea Scrolls, first discovered in the caves near Qumran in 1947, detail the rules of the community life of the Essenes. It is possible that John the Baptist, son of Zechariah and Elizabeth and cousin to Jesus, was influenced by the desert asceticism of the Essenes, who lived very near the Jordan River, where he administered his baptism of repentance.

Life of Jesus: Desert Sojourn

ca. 27 A.D. At the beginning of Jesus' public life, after his baptism in the River Jordan by John, he went into the desert alone to pray. Accounts are given in the Gospels of Matthew (4:1–11), Mark (1:12–13), and Luke (4:1–12), of Jesus' solitary forty-day retreat. There he fasted, prayed, and endured temptations by Satan, who tried to seduce him with promises of material power and prosperity if he would only disobey God and worship Satan instead. Jesus refused Satan and affirmed his obedience to the will of his Father.

Jesus was tested in ways analogous to the testing of Israel during the wandering in the desert after the escape from slavery in Egypt. Moses spent forty days on Mount Sinai, where he received the revelation of the Ten Commandments from God. In the desert, Israel was asked to affirm obedience in faith to Yahweh, who manifested Himself as the one, true God, and gave His law as a guide. The Israelites were repeatedly tempted to abandon Yahweh for pagan idol worship before their arrival in the Promised Land, a paradigm of Heaven.

Primitive Christian Spirituality and Asceticism

1st–4th Centuries, A.D. Early Christian, pre-monastic spirituality included fasting, voluntary celibacy, community prayer, and simple living. Wealth and security in this life were eschewed by ardent followers as a way of identifying with the sufferings of the poor Christ. Renunciation of the things of this world allowed devout Christians to focus their hearts and minds on the Kingdom of God and the Second Coming of Christ.

Members of the primitive Church gathered together for the eucharistic supper, which included homilies on Scripture readings and prayers. These early years of the Church were marked by persecution. To accept Baptism was to incur the risk of martyrdom. To die in the name of Christ and for His sake was to imitate Him with the totality of one's being.

Persecution ceased under Constantine the Great (285–337), the Roman emperor who was converted to Christianity through the influence of his mother, St. Helena. By the fourth century, peace and security allowed a certain political and material worldliness to influence Christian life. This, in turn, gave rise to the impetus to flee society for the desert by those who yearned for a purer, more intense experience of prayer and asceticism.

Early Christian Monasticism

251–356 A.D. St. Antony of Egypt heard the Gospel call to give all his possessions to the poor and so disposed of his wealth and retired to the desert in 285, determined not to let the desire for possessions rule his life. He became known as the "father of all monks" when St. Athanasius, who was bishop of Alexandria in Egypt, wrote his biography. This document of primitive monastic life details the asceticism of evangelical perfection: withdrawal from the world, renunciation, solitude, work, and prayer, which are the foundation of the monk's life even today. This description of anchoritic (solitary) monastic life was translated into Latin *(Vita Antonii)* and became well-known and influential in the West.

ca. 290–346 A.D. St. Pachomius was an Egyptian abbot who founded cenobitic monasticism, which is characterized by a strict common life. The *Rule of St. Pachomius,* translated into Latin ca. 404 A.D. by St. Jerome, contains directives for living a life in common inspired by the fellowship of Christians in the Eucharist, such as was found in very early Christianity. This rule had a great influence on succeeding forms of Western monasticism.

329?–79 A.D. St. Basil the Great was influenced by Pachomius. He founded monastic communities in Cappadocia (eastern Asia Minor) that were oriented to a life in common and for which he wrote his own Rule. The Basilian ideal survives, somewhat transmuted, in *The Rule of St. Benedict.*

330–90 A.D. St. Gregory of Nazianzen, friend of St. Basil and one of the Cappadocian Fathers of the Church, contributed through his theology the spiritual asceticism that informed Basil's Rule. The asceticism of consecrated virginity, and the poverty and solitude which are concomitant with it, enable the Christian to identify with the crucified Christ and to express complete fidelity to Him.

332–94 A.D. St. Gregory of Nyssa, brother of St. Basil and third of the "three great Cappadocians," wrote profoundly mystical works, e.g., the *Life of Moses,* in which he advocated a return to a state of original purity or perfection through a life of virtue lived in cooperation with the work of the Spirit within us. This synergy brings about a restoration of our true freedom as created in the image and likeness of God.

397 A.D. The year of St. Martin of Tours' death; he was the founder of the first monastery in Gaul at Liguge. He was made bishop of Tours in 371. Even as bishop he lived as a monk.

ca. 334–397 A.D. St. Ambrose, a Doctor of the Latin Church, was made bishop of Milan in 374. He gave all his property away to the poor, lived a life of personal asceticism, consecrated virgins, and was the spiritual father of a monastery very near Milan. It was at Milan that St. Augustine, who was greatly influenced by Ambrose, first heard of monastic life.

ca. 347–419 A.D. St. Jerome was a scripture scholar and a Doctor of the Latin Church. In addition to his great scholarship and many writings, Jerome, together with the wealthy widow Paula, founded monasteries in the Holy Land for both men and women, where he and Paula spent the rest of their lives.

354–430 A.D.   St. Augustine of Hippo, Doctor of the Latin Church, brought monastic life to Africa. Augustine wrote a monastic rule widely used today by both male and female communities. The hallmarks of his rule are charity, discretion, and community living, stressing common ownership of property, a widespread custom that is still current. It was this rule that influenced Western monasticism into the fifth century and paved the way for St. Benedict.

ca. 360–ca. 435 A.D.   St. John Cassian lived as a monk, a priest, and a spiritual writer. He founded two monasteries in Marseilles, one for men and one for women, around 415 A.D. His *Institutes* describe the external observances for monastic life. His other writings exhort religious perfection.

480–546 A.D.   St. Benedict of Nursia lived an eremitic monastic life for a time in Subiaco, Italy. In response to the many disciples who came to seek him out, Benedict set up cenobitic monastic groups. He then founded a Grand Monastery at Monte Cassino, where he wrote his Rule around 530. The defining characteristic of *The Rule of St. Benedict* is prayer, both personal and communal, issuing from the reading *(lectio divina)* of Scripture and the Fathers of the Church. The *opus Dei* of Benedictine life is the celebration of the Eucharist and the chanting of the Divine Office.

540–604 A.D.   St. Gregory the Great, Pope, was the last of the four great Latin Doctors of the Church. Before becoming pope, he founded monasteries in Sicily, and he himself lived under the Benedictine Rule. As pope, he sent St. Augustine, a fellow monk, to the Anglo-Saxons in 596. Augustine became archbishop of Canterbury in 597, where he set up a monastic chapter. St. Gregory the Great was an enthusiastic promoter of monasticism. He wrote on the life and miracles of St. Benedict, a work that became very popular and influential in the medieval era.

Through St. Benedict and St. Gregory the Great, the Church and the culture of antiquity were guided safely into the era now called the Middle Ages.

The Rule *of*

St. Benedict

PROLOGUE

Listen carefully, my son, to the master's instructions, and attend to them with the ear of your heart. This is advice from a father who loves you; welcome it, and faithfully put it into practice. The labor of obedience will bring you back to him from whom you had drifted through the sloth of disobedience. This message of mine is for you, then, if you are ready to give up your own will, once and for all, and armed with the strong and noble weapons of obedience to do battle for the true King, Christ the Lord.

First of all, every time you begin a good work, you must pray to him most earnestly to bring it to perfection. In his goodness, he has already counted us as his sons, and therefore we should never grieve him by our evil actions. With his good gifts which are in us, we must obey him at all times that he may never become the angry father who disinherits his sons, nor the dread lord, enraged by our sins, who punishes us forever as worthless servants for refusing to follow him to glory.

Let us get up then, at long last, for the Scriptures rouse us when they say: *It is high time for us to arise from sleep.*[1] Let us open our eyes to the light that comes from God, and our ears to the voice from heaven that every day calls out this charge: *If you hear his voice today, do not harden your hearts.*[2] And again: *You that have ears to hear, listen to what the Spirit says to the churches.*[3] And what does he say? *Come and listen to me, sons; I will teach you the fear of the Lord.*[4] *Run while you have the light* of life, *that the darkness* of death *may not overtake you.*[5]

Seeking his workman in a multitude of people, the Lord calls out to him and lifts his voice again: *Is there anyone here who yearns for life and desires to see good days?*[6] If you hear this and your answer is "I do," God then directs these words to you: If you desire true and eternal life, *keep your tongue free from vicious talk and your lips from all deceit; turn away from evil and do good; let peace be your quest and aim.*[7] Once you have done this, my *eyes will be upon* you *and* my *ears will listen* for your *prayers; and even before you ask me, I will say* to you: *Here I am.*[8] What, dear brothers, is more delightful than this voice of the Lord calling to us? See how the Lord in his love shows us the way of life. Clothed then with faith and the performance of good works, let us set out on this way, with the Gospel for our guide, that we may deserve to see him *who has called* us *to his kingdom.*[9]

If we wish to dwell in the tent of this kingdom, we will never arrive unless we run there by doing good deeds. But let us ask the Lord with the Prophet; *Who will dwell in your tent, Lord; who will find rest upon your holy mountain?*[10] After this question, brothers, let us listen well to what the Lord says in reply, for he shows us the way to his tent. *One who walks without blemish,* he says, *and is just in all his dealings; who speaks the truth from his heart and has not practiced deceit with his tongue; who has not wronged a fellowman in any way, nor listened to slanders against his neighbor.*[11] He has *foiled* the *evil one,* the devil, at every turn, flinging both him and his promptings far *from the sight* of his heart. While these temptations were still *young, he caught hold of them and dashed them against* Christ.[12] These people *fear the Lord,* and do not become elated over their good deeds; they judge it is the Lord's power, not their own, that brings about the good in them. *They praise*[13] the Lord working in them, and say with the Prophet: *Not to us, Lord, not to us give the glory, but to your name alone.*[14] In just this way Paul the

Apostle refused to take credit for the power of his preaching. He declared: *By God's grace I am what I am.*[15] And again he said: *He who boasts should make his boast in the Lord.*[16] That is why the Lord says in the Gospel: *Whoever hears these words of mine and does them is like a wise man who built his house upon rock; the floods came and the winds blew and beat against the house, but it did not fall: it was founded on rock.*[17]

With this conclusion, the Lord waits for us daily to translate into action, as we should, his holy teachings. Therefore our life span has been lengthened by way of a truce, that we may amend our misdeeds. As the Apostle says: *Do you not know that the patience of God is leading you to repent?*[18] And indeed the Lord assures us in his love: *I do not wish the death of the sinner, but that he turn back to me and live.*[19]

Brothers, now that we have asked the Lord who will dwell in his tent, we have heard the instruction for dwelling in it, but only if we fulfill the obligations of those who live there. We must, then, prepare our hearts and bodies for the battle of holy obedience to his instructions. What is not possible to us by nature, let us ask the Lord to supply by the help of his grace. If we wish to reach eternal life, even as we avoid the torments of hell, then—while there is still time, while we are in this body and have time to accomplish all these things by the light of life—we must run and do now what will profit us forever.

Therefore we intend to establish a school for the Lord's service. In drawing up its regulations, we hope to set down nothing harsh, nothing burdensome. The good of all concerned, however, may prompt us to a little strictness in order to amend faults and to safeguard love. Do not be daunted immediately by fear and run away from the road that leads to salvation. It is bound to be narrow at the outset. But as we progress in this way of life and in faith, we shall run on the path of God's commandments, our hearts over-flowing with the inexpressible delight of love. Never swerving from his instructions, then, but faithfully observing his teaching in the monastery until death, we shall through patience share in the sufferings of Christ that we may deserve also to share in his kingdom. Amen.

[It is called a rule because it regulates the lives of those who obey it]

Chapter 1

THE KINDS OF MONKS

There are clearly four kinds of monks. First, there are the cenobites, that is to say, those who belong to a monastery, where they serve under a rule and an abbot.

Second, there are the anchorites or hermits, who have come through the test of living in a monastery for a long time, and have passed beyond the first fervor of monastic life. Thanks to the help and guidance of many, they are now trained to fight against the devil. They have built up their strength and go from the battle line in the ranks of their brothers to the single combat of the desert. Self-reliant now, without the support of another, they are ready with God's help to grapple single-handed with the vices of body and mind.

Third, there are the sarabaites, the most detestable kind of monks, who, with no experience to guide them, no rule to try them *as gold is tried in a furnace,*[20] have a character as soft as lead. Still loyal to the world by their actions, they clearly lie to God by their tonsure. Two or three together, or even alone, without a shepherd, they pen themselves up in their own sheepfolds, not the Lord's. Their law is what they like to do, whatever strikes their fancy. Anything they believe in and choose, they call holy; anything they dislike, they consider forbidden.

Fourth and finally, there are the monks called gyrovagues, who spend their entire lives drifting from region to region, staying as guests for three or four days in different monasteries. Always on the move, they never settle down, and are slaves to their own wills and gross appetites. In every way they are worse than sarabaites.

It is better to keep silent than to speak of all these and their disgraceful way of life. Let us pass them by, then, and with the help of the Lord, proceed to draw up a plan for the strong kind, the cenobites.

Chapter 2

QUALITIES OF THE ABBOT

To be worthy of the task of governing a monastery, the abbot must always remember what his title signifies and act as a superior should. He is believed to hold the place of Christ in the monastery, since he is addressed by a title of Christ, as the Apostle indicates: *You have received the spirit of adoption of sons by which we exclaim, abba, father.*[21] Therefore, the abbot must never teach or decree or command anything that would deviate from the Lord's instructions. On the contrary, everything he teaches and commands should, like the leaven of divine justice, permeate the minds of his disciples. Let the abbot always remember that at the fearful judgment of God, not only his teaching but also his disciples' obedience will come under scrutiny. The abbot must, therefore, be aware that the shepherd will bear the blame wherever the father of the household finds that the sheep have yielded no profit. Still, if he has faithfully shepherded a restive and disobedient flock, always striving to cure their unhealthy ways, it will be otherwise: the shepherd will be acquitted at the Lord's judgment. Then, like the Prophet, he may say to the Lord: *I have not hidden your justice in my heart; I have proclaimed you truth and your salvation,*[22] *but they spurned and rejected me.*[23] Then at last the sheep that have rebelled against his care will be punished by the overwhelming power of death.

Furthermore, anyone who receives the name of abbot is to lead his disciples by a twofold teaching: he must point out to them all that is good and holy more by example than by words, proposing the commandments of the Lord to receptive disciples with words, but demonstrating God's instructions to the stubborn and the dull by a living example. Again, if he teaches his disciples that something is not to be done, then neither must he do it, *lest after preaching to others, he himself be found reprobate*[24] and God some day call to him in his sin: *How is it that you repeat my just commands and mouth my covenant when you hate discipline and toss my words behind you?*[25] And also this: *How is it that you can see a splinter in your brother's eye, and never notice the plank in your own?*[26] The abbot should avoid all favoritism in the monastery. He is not to love one more than another unless he finds someone better in good actions and obedience. A man born free is not to be given higher rank than a slave who becomes a monk, except for some other good reason. But the abbot is free, if he sees fit, to change anyone's rank as justice demands. Ordinarily, everyone is to keep to his regular place, because *whether slave or free, we are all one in Christ*[27] and share alike in bearing arms in the service of the one Lord, for *God shows no partiality among persons.*[28] Only in this are we distinguished in his sight: if we are found better than others in good works and in humility. Therefore, the abbot is to show equal love to everyone and apply the same discipline to all according to their merits.

In his teaching, the abbot should always observe the Apostle's recommendation, in which he says: *Use argument, appeal, reproof.*[29] This means that he must vary with circumstances, threatening and coaxing by turns, stern as a taskmaster, devoted and tender as only a father can be. With the undisciplined and restless, he will use firm argument; with the obedient and docile and patient, he will appeal for greater virtue; but as for the negligent and disdainful, we charge him to use reproof and rebuke. He should not gloss over the sins of those who err, but cut them out while he can, as soon as they begin to sprout, remembering the fate of Eli, priest of Shiloh.[30] For upright and perceptive men, his first and second warnings should be verbal; but those who are evil or stubborn, arrogant or disobedient, he can curb only by blows or some other physical punishment at the first offense. It is written, *The fool cannot be corrected with words;*[31] and again, *Strike your son with a rod and you will free his soul from death.*[32]

The abbot must always remember what he is and remember what he is called, aware that more will be expected of a man to whom more has been entrusted. He must know what a difficult and demanding burden he has undertaken: directing souls and serving a variety of temperaments, coaxing, reproving and encouraging them as appropriate. He must so accommodate and adapt himself to each one's character and intelligence that he will not only keep the flock entrusted to his care from dwindling, but will rejoice in the increase of a good flock. Above all, he must not show too great concern for the fleeting and temporal things of this world, neglecting or treating lightly the welfare of those entrusted to him. Rather, he should keep in mind that he has undertaken the care of souls for whom he must give an account. That he may not plead lack of resources as an excuse, he is to remember what is written: *Seek first the kingdom of God and his justice, and all these things will be given you as well,*[33] and again, *Those who fear him lack nothing.*[34]

The abbot must know that anyone undertaking the charge of souls must be ready to account for them. Whatever the number of brothers he has in his care, let him realize that on judgment day he will surely have to submit a reckoning to the Lord for all their souls—and indeed for his own as well. In this way, while always fearful of the future examination of the shepherd about the sheep entrusted to him and careful about the state of others' accounts, he becomes concerned also about his own, and while helping others to amend by his warnings, he achieves the amendment of his own faults.

Chapter 3
SUMMONING THE BROTHERS
FOR COUNSEL

As often as anything important is to be done in the monastery, the abbot shall call the whole community together and himself explain what the business is; and after hearing the advice of the brothers, let him ponder it and follow what he judges the wiser course. The reason why we have said all should be called for counsel is that the Lord often reveals what is better to the younger. The brothers, for their part, are to express their opinions with all humility, and not presume to defend their own views obstinately. The decision is rather the abbot's to make, so that when he has determined what is more prudent, all may obey. Nevertheless, just as it is proper for disciples to obey their master, so it is becoming for the master on his part to settle everything with foresight and fairness.

Accordingly in every instance, all are to follow the teaching of the rule, and no one shall rashly deviate from it. In the monastery no one is to follow his own heart's desire, nor shall anyone presume to contend with his abbot defiantly, or outside the monastery. Should anyone presume to do so, let him be subjected to the discipline of the rule. Moreover, the abbot himself must fear God and keep the rule in everything he does; he can be sure beyond any doubt that he will have to give an account of all his judgments to God, the most just of judges.

If less important business of the monastery is to be transacted, he shall take counsel with the seniors only, as it is written: *Do everything with counsel and you will not be sorry afterward.*[35]

Chapter 4

THE TOOLS FOR GOOD WORKS

First of all, *love the Lord God with your whole heart, your whole soul and all your strength, and love your neighbor as yourself.*[36] Then the following: *You are not to kill, not to commit adultery; you are not to steal nor to covet,*[37] *you are not to bear false witness.*[38] *You must honor everyone,*[39] and *never do to another what you do not want done to yourself.*[40]

Renounce yourself in order to follow Christ;[41] *discipline your body;*[42] do not pamper yourself, but love fasting. You must relieve the lot of the poor, *clothe the naked, visit the sick,*[43] and bury the dead. Go to help the troubled and console the sorrowing.

Your way of acting should be different from the world's way; the love of Christ must come before all else. You are not to act in anger or nurse a grudge. Rid your heart of all deceit. Never give a hollow greeting of peace or turn away when someone needs your love. Bind yourself to no oath lest it prove false, but speak the truth with heart and tongue.

Do not repay one bad turn with another.[44] Do not injure anyone, but bear injuries patiently. *Love your enemies.*[45] If people curse you, do not curse them back but bless them instead. *Endure perse-cution for the sake of justice.*[46]

You must *not* be *proud, nor be given to wine.*[47] Refrain from too much eating or sleeping, and *from laziness.*[48] Do not grumble or speak ill of others.

Place your hope in God alone. If you notice something good in yourself, give credit to God, not to yourself, but be certain that the evil you commit is always your own and yours to acknowledge.

Live in fear of judgment day and have a great horror of hell. Yearn for everlasting life with holy desire. Day by day remind yourself that you are going to die. Hour by hour keep careful watch over all you do, aware that God's gaze is upon you, wher-ever you may be. As soon as wrongful thoughts come into your heart, dash them against Christ and disclose them to your spiri-tual father. Guard your lips from harmful or deceptive speech. Prefer moderation in speech and speak no foolish chatter, nothing just to provoke laughter; do not love immoderate or boisterous laughter.

Listen readily to holy reading, and devote yourself often to prayer. Every day with tears and sighs confess your past sins to God in prayer and change from these evil ways in the future.

Do not gratify the promptings of the flesh;[49] hate the urgings of self-will. Obey the orders of the abbot unreservedly, even if his own conduct—which God forbid—be at odds with what he says. Remember the teaching of the Lord: *Do what they say, not what they do.*[50]

Do not aspire to be called holy before you really are, but first be holy that you may more truly be called so. Live by God's com-mandments every day; treasure chastity, harbor neither hatred nor jealousy of anyone, and do nothing out of envy. Do not love quarreling; shun arrogance. Respect the elders and love the young. Pray for your enemies out of love for Christ. If you have a dispute with someone, make peace with him before the sun goes down.

And finally, never lose hope in God's mercy.

These, then, are the tools of the spiritual craft. When we have used them without ceasing, day and night, and have returned them on judgment day, our wages will be the reward the Lord has promised: *What the eye has not seen nor the ear heard, God has prepared for those who love him.*[51] The workshop where we are to toil faithfully at all these tasks is the enclosure of the monastery and stability in the community.

Chapter 5

OBEDIENCE

The first step of humility is unhesitating obedience, which comes naturally to those who cherish Christ above all. Because of the holy service they have professed, or because of dread of hell and for the glory of everlasting life, they carry out the superior's order as promptly as if the command came from God himself. The Lord says of men like this: *No sooner did he hear than he obeyed me;*[52] again, he tells teachers: *Whoever listens to you, listens to me.*[53] Such people as these immediately put aside their own concerns, abandon their own will, and lay down whatever they have in hand, leaving it unfinished. With the ready step of obedience, they follow the voice of authority in their actions. Almost at the same moment, then, as the master gives the instruction the disciple quickly puts it into practice in the fear of God; and both actions together are swiftly completed as one.

It is love that impels them to pursue everlasting life; therefore, they are eager to take the narrow road of which the Lord says: *Narrow is the road that leads to life.*[54] They no longer live by their own judgment, giving in to their whims and appetites; rather they walk according to another's decisions and directions, choosing to live in monasteries and to have an abbot over them. Men of this resolve unquestionably conform to the saying of the Lord: *I have come not to do my own will, but the will of him who sent me.*[55]

This very obedience, however, will be acceptable to God and agreeable to men only if compliance with what is commanded is not cringing or sluggish or halfhearted, but free from any grumbling or any reaction of unwillingness. For the obedience shown to superiors is given to God, as he himself said: *Whoever listens to you, listens to me.*[56] Furthermore, the disciples' obedience must be given gladly, for *God loves a cheerful giver.*[57] If a disciple obeys grudgingly and grumbles, not only aloud but also in his heart, then, even though he carries out the order, his action will not be accepted with favor by God, who sees that he is grumbling in his heart. He will have no reward for service of this kind; on the contrary, he will incur punishment for grumbling, unless he changes for the better and makes amends.

Chapter 6
RESTRAINT OF SPEECH

Let us follow the Prophet's counsel: *I said, I have resolved to keep watch over my ways that I may never sin with my tongue. I have put a guard on my mouth. I was silent and was humbled, and I refrained even from good words.*[58] Here the Prophet indicates that there are times when good words are to be left unsaid out of esteem for silence. For all the more reason, then, should evil speech be curbed so that punishment for sin may be avoided. Indeed, so important is silence that permission to speak should seldom be granted even to mature disciples, no matter how good or holy or constructive their talk, because it is written: *In a flood of words you will not avoid sin;*[59] and elsewhere, *The tongue holds the key to life and death.*[60] Speaking and teaching are the master's task; the disciple is to be silent and listen.

Therefore, any requests to a superior should be made with all humility and respectful submission. We absolutely condemn in all places any vulgarity and gossip and talk leading to laughter, and we do not permit a disciple to engage in words of that kind.

Chapter 7

HUMILITY

Brothers, divine Scripture calls to us, saying: *Whoever exalts himself shall be humbled, and whoever humbles himself shall be exalted.*[61] In saying this, therefore, it shows us that every exaltation is a kind of pride, which the Prophet indicates he has shunned, saying: *Lord, my heart is not exalted; my eyes are not lifted up and I have not walked in the ways of the great nor gone after marvels beyond me.*[62] And why? *If I had not a humble spirit, but were exalted instead, then you would treat me like a weaned child on its mother's lap.*[63]

Accordingly, brothers, if we want to reach the highest summit of humility, if we desire to attain speedily that exaltation in heaven to which we climb by the humility of this present life, then by our ascending actions we must set up that ladder on which Jacob in a dream saw *angels descending and ascending.*[64] Without doubt, this descent and ascent can signify only that we descend by exaltation and ascend by humility. Now the ladder erected is our life on earth, and if we humble our hearts the Lord will raise it to heaven. We may call our body and soul the sides of this ladder, into which our divine vocation has fitted the various steps of humility and discipline as we ascend.

The first step of humility, then, is that a man keeps the *fear of God* always *before his eyes*[65] and never forgets it. He must constantly remember everything God has commanded, keeping in mind that all who despise God will burn in hell for their sins, and all who fear God have everlasting life awaiting them. While he guards himself at every moment from sins and vices of thought or tongue, of hand or foot, of self-will or bodily desire, let him recall that he is always seen by God in heaven, that his actions everywhere are in God's sight and are reported by angels at every hour.

The Prophet indicates this to us when he shows that our thoughts are always present to God, saying: *God searches hearts and minds;*[66] again he says: *The Lord knows the thoughts of men;*[67] likewise, *From afar you know my thoughts;*[68] and, *The thoughts of man shall give you praise.*[69] That he may take care to avoid sinful thoughts, the virtuous brother must always say to himself: *I shall be blameless in his sight* if *I guard myself from my own wickedness.*[70]

Truly, we are forbidden to do our own will, for Scripture tells us: *Turn away from your desires.*[71] And in the Prayer too we ask God that his *will be done* in us.[72] We are rightly taught not to do our own will, since we dread what Scripture says: *There are ways which men call right that in the end plunge into the depths of hell.*[73] Moreover, we fear what is said of those who ignore this: *They are corrupt and have become depraved in their desires.*[74]

As for the desires of the body, we must believe that God is always with us, for *All my desires are known to you,*[75] as the Prophet tells the Lord. We must then be on guard against any base desire, because death is stationed near the gateway of pleasure. For this reason Scripture warns us, *Pursue not your lusts.*[76]

Accordingly, if *the eyes of the Lord are watching the good and the wicked,*[77] *if at all times the Lord looks down from heaven on the sons of men to see whether any understand and seek God;*[78] and if every day the angels assigned to us report our deeds to the Lord day and night, then, brothers, we must be vigilant every hour or, as the Prophet says in the psalm, God may observe us *falling* at some time into evil and *so made worthless.*[79] After sparing us for a while because he is a loving father who waits for us to improve, he may tell us later, *This you did, and I said nothing.*[80]

The second step of humility is that a man loves not his own will nor takes pleasure in the satisfaction of his desires; rather he shall imitate by his actions that saying of the Lord: *I have come not to do my own will, but the will of him who sent me.*[81] Similarly we read, "Consent merits punishment; constraint wins a crown."

The third step of humility is that a man submits to his superior in all obedience for the love of God, imitating the Lord, of whom the Apostle says: *He became obedient even to death.*[82]

The fourth step of humility is that in this obedience under difficult, unfavorable, or even unjust conditions, his heart quietly embraces suffering and endures it without weakening or seeking escape. For Scripture has it: *Anyone who perseveres to the end will be saved,*[83] and again, *Be brave of heart and rely on the Lord.*[84] Another passage shows how the faithful must endure everything, even contradiction, for the Lord's sake, saying in the person of those who suffer, *For your sake we are put to death continually; we are regarded as sheep marked for slaughter.*[85] They are so confident in their expectation of reward from God that they continue joyfully and say, *But in all this we overcome because of him who so greatly loved us.*[86] Elsewhere Scripture says: *O God, you have tested us, you have tried us as silver is tried by fire; you have led us into a snare, you have placed afflictions on our backs.*[87] Then, to show that we ought to be under a superior, it adds: *You have placed men over our heads.*[88]

In truth, those who are patient amid hardships and unjust treatment are fulfilling the Lord's command: *When struck on one cheek, they turn the other; when deprived of their coat, they offer their cloak also; when pressed into service for one mile, they go two.*[89] With the Apostle Paul, they bear with *false brothers, endure persecution,* and *bless those who curse them.*[90]

The fifth step of humility is that a man does not conceal from his abbot any sinful thoughts entering his heart, or any wrongs committed in secret, but rather confesses them humbly. Concerning this, Scripture exhorts us: *Make known your way to the Lord and hope in him.*[91] And again, *Confess to the Lord, for he is good; his mercy is forever.*[92] So too the Prophet: *To you I have acknowledged my offense; my faults I have not concealed. I have said: Against myself I will report my faults to the Lord, and you have forgiven the wickedness of my heart.*[93]

The sixth step of humility is that a monk is content with the lowest and most menial treatment, and regards himself as a poor and worthless workman in whatever task he is given, saying to himself with the Prophet: *I am insignificant and ignorant, no better than a beast before you, yet I am with you always.*[94]

The seventh step of humility is that a man not only admits with his tongue but is also convinced in his heart that he is inferior to all and of less value, humbling himself and saying with the Prophet: *I am truly a worm, not a man, scorned by men and despised by the people.*[95] *I was exalted, then I was humbled and overwhelmed with confusion.*[96] And again, *It is a blessing that you have humbled me so that I can learn your commandments.*[97]

The eighth step of humility is that a monk does only what is endorsed by the common rule of the monastery and the example set by his superiors.

The ninth step of humility is that a monk controls his tongue and remains silent, not speaking unless asked a question, for Scripture warns, *In a flood of words you will not avoid sinning,*[98] and, *A talkative man goes about aimlessly on earth.*[99]

The tenth step of humility is that he is not given to ready laughter, for it is written: *Only a fool raises his voice in laughter.*[100]

The eleventh step of humility is that a monk speaks gently and without laughter, seriously and with becoming modesty, briefly and reasonably, but without raising his voice, as it is written: "A wise man is known by his few words."

The twelfth step of humility is that a monk always manifests humility in his bearing no less than in his heart, so that it is evident at the Work of God, in the oratory, the monastery or the garden, on a journey or in the field, or anywhere else. Whether he sits, walks or stands, his head must be bowed and his eyes cast down. Judging himself always guilty on account of his sins, he should consider that he is already at the fearful judgment, and constantly say in his heart what the publican in the Gospel said with downcast eyes: *Lord, I am a sinner, not worthy to look up to heaven.*[101] And with the Prophet: *I am bowed down and humbled in every way.*[102]

Now, therefore, after ascending all these steps of humility, the monk will quickly arrive at that *perfect love* of God which *casts out fear.*[103] Through this love, all that he once performed with dread, he will now begin to observe without effort, as though naturally, from habit, no longer out of fear of hell, but out of love for Christ, good habit and delight in virtue. All this the Lord will by the Holy Spirit graciously manifest in his workman now cleansed of vices and sins.

Chapter 8

THE DIVINE OFFICE AT NIGHT

During the winter season, that is, from the first of November until Easter, it seems reasonable to arise at the eighth hour of the night. By sleeping until a little past the middle of the night, the brothers can arise with their food fully digested. In the time remaining after Vigils, those who need to learn some of the psalter or readings should study them.

Between Easter and the first of November mentioned above, the time for Vigils should be adjusted so that a very short interval after Vigils will give the monks opportunity to care for nature's needs. Then, at daybreak, Lauds should follow immediately.

Chapter 9

THE NUMBER OF PSALMS
AT THE NIGHT OFFICE

During the winter season, Vigils begin with the verse: *Lord, open my lips and my mouth shall proclaim your praise.*[104] After this has been said three times, the following order is observed: Psalm 3 with "Glory be to the Father"; Psalm 94 with a refrain, or at least chanted; an Ambrosian hymn; then six psalms with refrain.

After the psalmody, a versicle is said and the abbot gives a blessing. When all are seated on the benches, the brothers in turn read three selections from the book on the lectern. After each reading a responsory is sung. "Glory be to the Father" is not sung after the first two responsories, but only after the third reading. As soon as the cantor begins to sing "Glory be to the Father," let all the monks rise from their seats in honor and reverence for the Holy Trinity. Besides the inspired books of the Old and New Testaments, the works read at Vigils should include explanations of Scripture by reputable and orthodox catholic Fathers.

When these three readings and their responsories have been finished, the remaining six psalms are sung with an "alleluia" refrain. This ended, there follow a reading from the Apostle recited by heart, a versicle and the litany, that is, "Lord, have mercy." And so Vigils are concluded.

Chapter 10

THE ARRANGEMENT OF THE NIGHT OFFICE IN SUMMER

From Easter until the first of November, the winter arrangement for the number of psalms is followed. But because summer nights are shorter, the readings from the book are omitted. In place of the three readings, one from the Old Testament is substituted. This is to be recited by heart, followed by a short responsory. In everything else, the winter arrangement for Vigils is kept. Thus, winter and summer, there are never fewer than twelve psalms at Vigils, not counting Psalms 3 and 94.

Chapter 11

THE CELEBRATION OF VIGILS ON SUNDAY

On Sunday the monks should arise earlier for Vigils. In these Vigils, too, there must be moderation in quantity: first, as we have already indicated, six psalms are said, followed by a versicle. Then the monks, seated on the benches and arranged in their proper order, listen to four readings from the book. After each reading a responsory is sung, but "Glory be to the Father" is added only to the fourth. When the cantor begins it, all immediately rise in reverence.

After these readings the same order is repeated: six more psalms with refrain as before, a versicle, then four more readings and their responsories, as above. Next, three canticles from the Prophets, chosen by the abbot, are said with an "alleluia" refrain. After a versicle and the abbot's blessing, four New Testament readings follow with their responsories, as above. After the fourth responsory, the abbot begins the hymn "We praise you, God." When that is finished, he reads from the Gospels while all the monks stand with respect and awe. At the conclusion of the Gospel reading, all reply "Amen," and immediately the abbot intones the hymn "To you be praise." After a final blessing, Lauds begin.

This arrangement for Sunday Vigils should be followed at all times, summer and winter, unless—God forbid—the monks happen to arise too late. In that case, the readings or responsories will have to be shortened. Let special care be taken that this not happen, but if it does, the monk at fault is to make due satisfaction to God in the oratory.

Chapter 12

THE CELEBRATION OF THE SOLEMNITY
OF LAUDS

Sunday Lauds begin with Psalm 66, said straight through without a refrain. Then Psalm 50 follows with an "alleluia" refrain. Lauds continue with Psalms 117 and 62, the Canticle of the Three Young Men, Psalms 148 through 150, a reading from the Apocalypse recited by heart and followed by a responsory, an Ambrosian hymn, a versicle, the Gospel Canticle, the litany and the conclusion.

Chapter 13
THE CELEBRATION OF LAUDS
ON ORDINARY DAYS

On ordinary weekdays, Lauds are celebrated as follows: First, Psalm 66 is said without a refrain and slightly protracted, as on Sunday, so that everyone can be present for Psalm 50, which has a refrain. Next, according to custom, two more psalms are said in the following order: on Monday, Psalms 5 and 35; on Tuesday, Psalms 42 and 56; on Wednesday, Psalms 63 and 64; on Thursday, Psalms 87 and 89; on Friday, Psalms 75 and 91; on Saturday, Psalm 142 and the Canticle from Deuteronomy, divided into two sections, with "Glory be to the Father" after each section. On other days, however, a Canticle from the Prophets is said, according to the practice of the Roman Church. Next follow Psalms 148 through 150, a reading from the Apostle recited by heart, a responsory, an Ambrosian hymn, a versicle, the Gospel Canticle, the litany and the conclusion.

Assuredly, the celebration of Lauds and Vespers must never pass by without the superior's reciting the entire Lord's Prayer at the end for all to hear, because thorns of contention are likely to spring up. Thus warned by the pledge they make to one another in the very words of this prayer: *Forgive us as we forgive,*[105] they may cleanse themselves of this kind of vice. At other celebrations, only the final part of the Lord's Prayer is said aloud, that all may reply: *But deliver us from evil.*[106]

Chapter 14

THE CELEBRATION OF VIGILS
ON THE ANNIVERSARIES OF SAINTS

On the feasts of saints, and indeed on all solemn festivals, the Sunday order of celebration is followed, although the psalms, refrains and readings proper to the day itself are said. The procedure, however, remains the same as indicated above.

Chapter 15

THE TIMES FOR SAYING ALLELUIA

From the holy feast of Easter until Pentecost, "alleluia" is always said with both the psalms and the responsories. Every night from Pentecost until the beginning of Lent, it is said only with the last six psalms of Vigils. Vigils, Lauds, Prime, Terce, Sext and None are said with "alleluia" every Sunday except in Lent; at Vespers, however, a refrain is used. "Alleluia" is never said with responsories except from Easter to Pentecost.

Chapter 16

THE CELEBRATION OF THE DIVINE
OFFICE DURING THE DAY

The Prophet says: *Seven times a day have I praised you.*[107] We will fulfill this sacred number of seven if we satisfy our obligations of service at Lauds, Prime, Terce, Sext, None, Vespers and Compline, for it was of these hours during the day that he said: *Seven times a day have I praised you.*[108] Concerning Vigils, the same Prophet says: *At midnight I arose to give you praise.*[109] Therefore, we should *praise* our Creator *for his just judgments* at these times: Lauds, Prime, Terce, Sext, None, Vespers and Compline; and *let us arise at night to give* him *praise*.[110]

Chapter 17

THE NUMBER OF PSALMS TO BE SUNG AT THESE HOURS

We have already established the order for psalmody at Vigils and Lauds. Now let us arrange the remaining hours.

Three psalms are to be said at Prime, each followed by "Glory be to the Father." The hymn for this hour is sung after the opening versicle, *God, come to my assistance,*[111] before the psalmody begins. One reading follows the three psalms, and the hour is concluded with a versicle, "Lord, have mercy" and the dismissal.

Prayer is celebrated in the same way at Terce, Sext and None: that is, the opening verse, the hymn appropriate to each hour, three psalms, a reading with a versicle, "Lord, have mercy" and the dismissal. If the community is rather large, refrains are used with the psalms; if it is smaller, the psalms are said without refrain.

At Vespers the number of psalms should be limited to four, with refrain. After these psalms there follow: a reading and responsory, an Ambrosian hymn, a versicle, the Gospel Canticle the litany, and, immediately before the dismissal, the Lord': Prayer.

Compline is limited to three psalms without refrain. After the psalmody comes the hymn for this hour, followed by a reading, versicle, "Lord, have mercy," a blessing and the dismissal.

Chapter 18
THE ORDER OF THE PSALMODY

Each of the day hours begins with the verse, *God, come to my assistance; Lord, make haste to help me,*[112] (Ps 69(70):2), followed by "Glory be to the Father" and the appropriate hymn.

Then, on Sunday at Prime, four sections of Psalm 118 are said. At the other hours, that is, at Terce, Sext and None, three sections of this psalm are said. On Monday three psalms are said at Prime: Psalms 1, 2 and 6. At Prime each day thereafter until Sunday, three psalms are said in consecutive order as far as Psalm 19. Psalms 9 and 17 are each divided into two sections. In this way, Sunday Vigils can always begin with Psalm 20.

On Monday at Terce, Sext and None, the remaining nine sections of Psalm 118 are said, three sections at each hour. Psalm 118 is thus completed in two days, Sunday and Monday. On Tuesday, three psalms are said at each of the hours of Terce, Sext and None. These are the nine psalms, 119 through 127. The same psalms are repeated at these hours daily up to Sunday. Likewise, the arrangement of hymns, readings and versicles for these days remains the same. In this way, Psalm 118 will always begin on Sunday.

Four psalms are sung each day at Vespers, starting with Psalm 109 and ending with Psalm 147, omitting the psalms in this series already assigned to other hours, namely, Psalms 117 through 127, Psalm 133 and Psalm 142. All the remaining psalms are said at Vespers. Since this leaves three psalms too few, the longer ones in the series should be divided: that is, Psalms 138, 143 and 144. And because Psalm 116 is short, it can be joined to Psalm 115. This is the order of psalms for Vespers; the rest is as arranged above: the reading, responsory, hymn, versicle and canticle.

The same psalms—4, 90 and 133—are said each day at Compline.

The remaining psalms not accounted for in this arrangement, for the day hours are distributed evenly at Vigils over the seven nights of the week. Longer psalms are to be divided so that twelve psalms are said each night.

Above all else we urge that if anyone finds this distribution of the psalms unsatisfactory, he should arrange whatever he judges better, provided that the full complement of one hundred and fifty psalms is by all means carefully maintained every week, and that the series begins anew each Sunday at Vigils. For monks who in a week's time say less than the full psalter with the customary canticles betray extreme indolence and lack of devotion in their service. We read, after all, that our holy Fathers, energetic as they were, did all this in a single day. Let us hope that we, lukewarm as we are, can achieve it in a whole week.

Chapter 19

THE DISCIPLINE OF PSALMODY

We believe that the divine presence is everywhere and *that in every place the eyes of the Lord are watching the good and the wicked.*[113] But beyond the least doubt we should believe this to be especially true when we celebrate the divine office.

We must always remember, therefore, what the Prophet says: *Serve the Lord with fear,*[114] and again, *Sing praise wisely;*[115] and, *In the presence of the angels I will sing to you.*[116] Let us consider, then, how we ought to behave in the presence of God and his angels, and let us stand to sing the psalms in such a way that our minds are in harmony with our voices.

Chapter 20

REVERENCE IN PRAYER

Whenever we want to ask some favor of a powerful man, we do it humbly and respectfully, for fear of presumption. How much more important, then, to lay our petitions before the Lord God of all things with the utmost humility and sincere devotion. We must know that God regards our purity of heart and tears of compunction, not our many words. Prayer should therefore be short and pure, unless perhaps it is prolonged under the inspiration of divine grace. In community, however, prayer should always be brief; and when the superior gives the signal, all should rise together.

Chapter 21

THE DEANS OF THE MONASTERY

If the community is rather large, some brothers chosen for their good repute and holy life should be made deans. They will take care of their groups of ten, managing all affairs according to the commandments of God and the orders of their abbot. The deans selected should be the kind of men with whom the abbot can confidently share the burdens of his office. They are to be chosen for virtuous living and wise teaching, not for their rank.

If perhaps one of these deans is found to be puffed up with any pride, and so deserving of censure, he is to be reproved once, twice and even a third time. Should he refuse to amend, he must be removed from office and replaced by another who is worthy. We prescribe the same course of action in regard to the prior.

Chapter 22

THE SLEEPING ARRANGEMENTS
OF THE MONKS

The monks are to sleep in separate beds. They receive bedding as provided by the abbot, suitable to monastic life.

If possible, all are to sleep in one place, but should the size of the community preclude this, they will sleep in groups of ten or twenty under the watchful care of seniors. A lamp must be kept burning in the room until morning.

They sleep clothed, and girded with belts of cords; but they should remove their knives, lest they accidentally cut themselves in their sleep. Thus the monks will always be ready to arise without delay when the signal is given; each will hasten to arrive at the Work of God before the others, yet with all dignity and decorum. The younger brothers should not have their beds next to each other, but interspersed among those of the seniors. On arising for the Work of God, they will quietly encourage each other, for the sleepy like to make excuses.

Chapter 23

EXCOMMUNICATION FOR FAULTS

If a brother is found to be stubborn or disobedient or proud, if he grumbles or in any way despises the holy rule and defies the orders of his seniors, he should be warned twice privately by the seniors, in accord with our Lord's injunction.[117] If he does not amend, he must be rebuked publicly in the presence of everyone. But if even then he does not reform, let him be excommunicated, provided that he understands the nature of this punishment. If, however, he lacks understanding, let him undergo corporal punishment.

Chapter 24
DEGREES OF EXCOMMUNICATION

There ought to be due proportion between the seriousness of a fault and the measure of excommunication or discipline. The abbot determines the gravity of faults.

If a brother is found guilty of less serious faults, he will not be allowed to share the common table. Anyone excluded from the common table will conduct himself as follows: in the oratory he will not lead a psalm or a refrain nor will he recite a reading until he has made satisfaction, and he will take his meals alone, after the brothers have eaten. For instance, if the brothers eat at noon, he will eat in midafternoon; if the brothers eat in midafternoon, he will eat in the evening, until by proper satisfaction he gains pardon.

Chapter 25
SERIOUS FAULTS

A brother guilty of a serious fault is to be excluded from both the table and the oratory. No other brother should associate or converse with him at all. He will work alone at the tasks assigned to him, living continually in sorrow and penance, pondering that fearful judgment of the Apostle: *Such a man is handed over for the destruction of his flesh, that his spirit may be saved on the day of the Lord.*[118] Let him take his food alone in an amount and at a time the abbot considers appropriate for him. He should not be blessed by anyone passing by, nor should the food that is given him be blessed.

Chapter 26

UNAUTHORIZED ASSOCIATION
WITH THE EXCOMMUNICATED

If a brother, acting without an order from the abbot, presumes to associate in any way with an excommunicated brother, to converse with him or to send him a message, he should receive a like punishment of excommunication.

Chapter 27

THE ABBOT'S CONCERN
FOR THE EXCOMMUNICATED

The abbot must exercise the utmost care and concern for wayward brothers, because *it is not the healthy who need a physician, but the sick.*[119] Therefore, he ought to use every skill of a wise physician and send in *senpectae,* that is, mature and wise brothers who, under the cloak of secrecy, may support the wavering brother, urge him to be humble as a way of making satisfaction, and *console* him *lest he be overwhelmed by excessive sorrow.*[120] Rather, as the Apostle also says: *Let love for him be reaffirmed,*[121] and let all pray for him.

It is the abbot's responsibility to have great concern and to act with all speed, discernment and diligence in order not to lose any of the sheep entrusted to him. He should realize that he has undertaken care of the sick, not tyranny over the healthy. Let him also fear the threat of the Prophet, in which God says: *What you saw to be fat you claimed for yourselves, and what was weak you cast aside.*[122] He is to imitate the loving example of the Good Shepherd who left the ninety-nine sheep in the mountains and went in search of the one sheep that had strayed. So great was his compassion for its weakness that *he* mercifully *placed it on his* sacred *shoulders* and so carried it back to the flock.[123]

Chapter 28

THOSE WHO REFUSE TO AMEND
AFTER FREQUENT REPROOFS

If a brother has been reproved frequently for any fault, or if he has even been excommunicated, yet does not amend, let him receive a sharper punishment: that is, let him feel the strokes of the rod. But if even then he does not reform, or perhaps becomes proud and would actually defend his conduct, which God forbids, the abbot should follow the procedure of a wise physician. After he has applied compresses, the ointment of encouragement, the medicine of divine Scripture, and finally the cauterizing iron of excommunication and strokes of the rod, and if he then perceives that his earnest efforts are unavailing, let him apply an even better remedy: he and all the brothers should pray for him so that the Lord, who can do all things, may bring about the health of the sick brother. Yet if even this procedure does not heal him, then finally, the abbot must use the knife and amputate. For the Apostle says: *Banish the evil one from your midst;*[124] and again, *If the unbeliever departs, let him depart,*[125] lest one diseased sheep infect the whole flock.

Chapter 29

READMISSION OF BROTHERS
WHO LEAVE THE MONASTERY

If a brother, following his own evil ways, leaves the monastery but then wishes to return, he must first promise to make full amends for leaving. Let him be received back, but as a test of his humility he should be given the last place. If he leaves again, or even a third time, he should be readmitted under the same conditions. After this, however, he must understand that he will be denied all prospect of return.

Chapter 30

THE MANNER OF REPROVING BOYS

Every age and level of understanding should receive appropriate treatment. Therefore, as often as boys and the young, or those who cannot understand the seriousness of the penalty of excommunication, are guilty of misdeeds, they should be subjected to severe fasts or checked with sharp strokes so that they may be healed.

Chapter 31

QUALIFICATIONS OF THE
MONASTERY CELLARER

As cellarer of the monastery, there should be chosen from the community someone who is wise, mature in conduct, temperate, not an excessive eater, not proud, excitable, offensive, dilatory or wasteful, but God-fearing, and like a father to the whole community. He will take care of everything, but will do nothing without an order from the abbot. Let him keep to his orders.

He should not annoy the brothers. If any brother happens to make an unreasonable demand of him, he should not reject him with disdain and cause him distress, but reasonably and humbly deny the improper request. Let him keep watch over his own soul, ever mindful of that saying of the Apostle: *He who serves well secures a good standing for himself.*[126] He must show every care and concern for the sick, children, guests and the poor, knowing for certain that he will be held accountable for all of them on the day of judgment. He will regard all utensils and goods of the monastery as sacred vessels of the altar, aware that nothing is to be neglected. He should not be prone to greed, nor be wasteful and extravagant with the goods of the monastery, but should do everything with moderation and according to the abbot's orders.

Above all, let him be humble. If goods are not available to meet a request, he will offer a kind word in reply, for it is written: *A kind word is better than the best gift.*[127] He should take care of all that the abbot entrusts to him, and not presume to do what the abbot has forbidden. He will provide the brothers their allotted amount of food without any pride or delay, lest they be led astray. For he must remember what the Scripture says that person deserves *who leads one of the little ones astray.*[128]

If the community is rather large, he should be given helpers, that with their assistance he may calmly perform the duties of his office. Necessary items are to be requested and given at the proper times, so that no one may be disquieted or distressed in the house of God.

Chapter 32

THE TOOLS AND GOODS
OF THE MONASTERY

The goods of the monastery, that is, its tools, clothing or anything else, should be entrusted to brothers whom the abbot appoints and in whose manner of life he has confidence. He will, as he sees fit, issue to them the various articles to be cared for and collected after use. The abbot will maintain a list of these, so that when the brothers succeed one another in their assigned tasks, he may be aware of what he hands out and what he receives back.

Whoever fails to keep the things belonging to the monastery clean or treats them carelessly should be reproved. If he does not amend, let him be subjected to the discipline of the rule.

Chapter 33

MONKS AND PRIVATE OWNERSHIP

Above all, this evil practice must be uprooted and removed from the monastery. We mean that, without an order from the abbot, no one may presume to give, receive or retain anything as his own, nothing at all—not a book, writing tablets or stylus—in short, not a single item, especially since monks may not have the free disposal even of their own bodies and wills. For their needs, they are to look to the father of the monastery, and are not allowed anything which the abbot has not given or permitted. *All things should be the common possession* of all, as it is written, *so that no one* presumes to *call anything his own.*[129]

But if anyone is caught indulging in this most evil practice, he should be warned a first and a second time. If he does not amend, let him be subjected to punishment.

Chapter 34
DISTRIBUTION OF GOODS ACCORDING TO NEED

It is written: *Distribution was made to each one as he had need.*[130] By this we do not imply that there should be favoritism—God forbid—but rather consideration for weaknesses. Whoever needs less should thank God and not be distressed, but whoever needs more should feel humble because of his weakness, not self-important because of the kindness shown him. In this way all the members will be at peace. First and foremost, there must be no word or sign of the evil of grumbling, no manifestation of it for any reason at all. If, however, anyone is caught grumbling, let him undergo more severe discipline.

Chapter 35
KITCHEN SERVERS OF THE WEEK

The brothers should serve one another. Consequently, no one will be excused from kitchen service unless he is sick or engaged in some important business of the monastery, for such service increases reward and fosters love. Let those who are not strong have help so that they may serve without distress, and let everyone receive help as the size of the community or local conditions warrant. If the community is rather large, the cellarer should be excused from kitchen service, and, as we have said, those should also be excused who are engaged in important business. Let all the rest serve one another in love.

On Saturday the brother who is completing his work will do the washing. He is to wash the towels which the brothers use to wipe their hands and feet. Both the one who is ending his service and the one who is about to begin are to wash the feet of everyone. The utensils required for the kitchen service are to be washed and returned intact to the cellarer, who in turn issues them to the one beginning his week. In this way the cellarer will know what he hands out and what he receives back.

An hour before mealtime, the kitchen workers of the week should each receive a drink and some bread over and above the regular portion, so that at mealtime, they may serve their brothers without grumbling or hardship. On solemn days, however, they should wait until after the dismissal.

On Sunday immediately after Lauds, those beginning as well as those completing their week of service should make a profound bow in the oratory before all and ask for their prayers. Let the server completing his week recite this verse: *Blessed are you, Lord God,* who *have helped me and comforted me.*[131] After this verse has been said three times, he receives a blessing. Then the one beginning his service follows and says: *God, come to my assistance; Lord, make haste to help me.*[132] And all repeat this verse three times. When he has received a blessing, he begins his service.

Chapter 36

THE SICK BROTHERS

Care of the sick must rank above and before all else, so that they may truly be served as Christ, for he said: *I was sick and you visited me,*[133] and, *What you did for one of these least brothers you did for me.*[134] Let the sick on their part bear in mind that they are served out of honor for God, and let them not by their excessive demands distress their brothers who serve them. Still, sick brothers must be patiently borne with, because serving them leads to a greater reward. Consequently, the abbot should be extremely careful that they suffer no neglect.

Let a separate room be designated for the sick, and let them be served by an attendant who is God-fearing, attentive and concerned. The sick may take baths whenever it is advisable, but the healthy, and especially the young, should receive permission less readily. Moreover, to regain their strength, the sick who are very weak may eat meat, but when their health improves, they should abstain from meat as usual.

The abbot must take the greatest care that cellarers and those who serve the sick do not neglect them, for the shortcomings of disciples are his responsibility.

Chapter 37

THE ELDERLY AND CHILDREN

Although human nature itself is inclined to be compassionate toward the old and the young, the authority of the rule should also provide for them. Since their lack of strength must always be taken into account, they should certainly not be required to follow the strictness of the rule with regard to food, but should be treated with kindly consideration and allowed to eat before the regular hours.

Chapter 38

THE READER FOR THE WEEK

Reading will always accompany the meals of the brothers. The reader should not be the one who just happens to pick up the book, but someone who will read for a whole week, beginning on

Sunday. After Mass and Communion, let the incoming reader ask all to pray for him so that God may shield him from the spirit of vanity. Let him begin this verse in the oratory: *Lord, open my lips, and my mouth shall proclaim your praise,*[135] and let all say it three times. When he has received a blessing, he will begin his week of reading.

Let there be complete silence. No whispering, no speaking— only the reader's voice should be heard there. The brothers should by turn serve one another's needs as they eat and drink, so that no one need ask for anything. If, however, anything is required, it should be requested by an audible signal of some kind rather than by speech. No one should presume to ask a question about the reading or about anything else, *lest occasion be given* [to the devil].[136] The superior, however, may wish to say a few words of instruction.

Because of holy Communion and because the fast may be too hard for him to bear, the brother who is reader for the week is to receive some diluted wine before he begins to read. Afterward he will take his meal with the weekly kitchen servers and the attendants.

Brothers will read and sing, not according to rank, but according to their ability to benefit their hearers.

Chapter 39
THE PROPER AMOUNT OF FOOD

For the daily meals, whether at noon or in midafternoon, it is enough, we believe, to provide all tables with two kinds of cooked food because of individual weaknesses. In this way, the person who may not be able to eat one kind of food may partake of the other. Two kinds of cooked food, therefore, should suffice for al the brothers, and if fruit or fresh vegetables are available, a third dish may also be added. A generous pound of bread is enough for a day, whether for only one meal or for both dinner and supper. In the latter case, the cellarer will set aside one third of this pound and give it to the brothers at supper.

Should it happen that the work is heavier than usual, the abbot may decide—and he will have the authority—to grant something additional, provided that it is appropriate, and that, above all, overindulgence is avoided, lest a monk experience indigestion. For nothing is so inconsistent with the life of any Christian as overindulgence. Our Lord says: *Take care that your hearts are not weighed down with overindulgence.*[137]

Young boys should not receive the same amount as their elders, but less, since in all matter frugality is the rule. Let everyone, except the sick who are very weak, abstain entirely from eating the meat of four-footed animals.

Chapter 40

THE PROPER AMOUNT OF DRINK

Everyone has his own gift from God, one this and another that.[138] It is, therefore, with some uneasiness that we specify the amount of food and drink for others. However, with due regard for the infirmities of the sick, we believe that a half bottle of wine a day is sufficient for each. But those to whom God gives the strength to abstain must know that they will earn their own reward.

The superior will determine when local conditions, work or the summer heat indicates the need for a greater amount. He must, in any case, take great care lest excess or drunkenness creep in. We read that monks should not drink wine at all, but since the monks of our day cannot be convinced of this, let us at least agree to drink moderately, and not to the point of excess, for *wine makes even wise men go astray.*[139]

However, where local circumstances dictate an amount much less than what is stipulated above, or even none at all, those who live there should bless God and not grumble. Above all else we admonish them to refrain from grumbling.

Chapter 41

THE TIMES FOR THE BROTHERS' MEALS

From holy Easter to Pentecost, the brothers eat at noon and take supper in the evening. Beginning with Pentecost and continuing throughout the summer, the monks fast until midafternoon on Wednesday and Friday, unless they are working in the fields or the summer heat is oppressive.

On the other days they eat dinner at noon. Indeed, the abbot may decide that they should continue to eat dinner at noon every day if they have work in the fields or if the summer heat remains extreme. Similarly, he should so regulate and arrange all matters that souls may be saved and the brothers may go about their activities without justifiable grumbling.

From the thirteenth of September to the beginning of Lent, they always take their meal in midafternoon. Finally, from the beginning of Lent to Easter, they eat towards evening. Let Vespers be celebrated early enough so that there is no need for a lamp while eating, and that everything can be finished by daylight. Indeed, at all times let supper or the hour of the fast-day meal be so scheduled that everything can be done by daylight.

Chapter 42

SILENCE AFTER COMPLINE

Monks should diligently cultivate silence at all times, but especially at night. Accordingly, this will always be the arrangement, whether for fast days or for ordinary days. When there are two meals, all the monks will sit together immediately after rising from supper. Someone should read from the *Conferences* or the *Lives* of the Fathers or at any rate something else that will benefit the hearers, but not the Heptateuch or the Books of Kings, because it will not be good for those of weak understanding to hear these writings at that hour; they should be read at other times.

On fast days there is to be a short interval between Vespers and the reading of the *Conferences,* as we have indicated. Then let four or five pages be read, or as many as time permits. This reading period will allow for all to come together, in case any were engaged in assigned tasks. When all have assembled, they should pray Compline; and on leaving Compline, no one will be permitted to speak further. If anyone is found to transgress this rule of silence, he must be subjected to severe punishment, except on occasions when guests require attention or the abbot wishes to give someone a command, but even this is to be done with the utmost seriousness and proper restraint.

Chapter 43

TARDINESS AT THE WORK OF GOD
OR AT TABLE

On hearing the signal for an hour of the divine office, the monk will immediately set aside what he has in hand and go with utmost speed, yet with gravity and without giving occasion for frivolity. Indeed, nothing is to be preferred to the Work of God.

If at Vigils anyone comes after the "Glory be to the Father" of Psalm 94, which we wish, therefore, to be said quite deliberately and slowly, he is not to stand in his regular place in choir. He must take the last place of all, or one set apart by the abbot for such offenders, that they may be seen by him and by all, until they do penance by public satisfaction at the end of the Work of God. We have decided, therefore, that they ought to stand either in the last place or apart from the others, so that the attention they attract will shame them into amending. Should they remain outside the oratory, there may be those who would return to bed and sleep, or, worse yet, settle down outside and engage in idle talk, thereby *giving occasion to the Evil One*.[140] They should come inside so that they will not lose everything and may amend in the future.

At the day hours the same rule applies to anyone who comes after the opening verse and the "Glory be to the Father" of the first psalm following it: he is to stand in the last place. Until he has made satisfaction, he is not to presume to join the choir of those praying the psalms, unless perhaps the abbot pardons him and grants an exception. Even in this case, the one at fault is still bound to satisfaction.

But if anyone does not come to table before the verse so that all may say the verse and pray and sit down at table together, and if this failure happens through the individual's own negligence or fault, he should be reproved up to the second time. If he still does not amend, let him not be permitted to share the common table, but take his meals alone, separated from the company of all. His portion of wine should be taken away until there is satisfaction and amendment. Anyone not present for the verse said after meals is to be treated in the same manner.

No one is to presume to eat or drink before or after the time appointed. Moreover, if anyone is offered something by a superior and refuses it, then, if later he wants what he refused or anything else, he should receive nothing at all until he has made appropriate amends.

Chapter 44
SATISFACTION
BY THE EXCOMMUNICATED

Anyone excommunicated for serious faults from the oratory and from the table is to prostrate himself in silence at the oratory entrance at the end of the celebration of the Work of God. He should lie face down at the feet of all as they leave the oratory, and let him do this until the abbot judges he has made satisfaction. Next, at the bidding of the abbot, he is to prostrate himself at the abbot's feet, then at the feet of all that they may pray for him. Only then, if the abbot orders, should he be admitted to the choir in the rank the abbot assigns. Even so, he should not presume to lead a psalm or a reading or anything else in the oratory without further instructions from the abbot. In addition, at all the hours, as the Work of God is being completed, he must prostrate himself in the place he occupies. He will continue this form of satisfaction until the abbot again bids him cease.

Those excommunicated for less serious faults from the table only are to make satisfaction in the oratory for as long as the abbot orders. They do so until he gives his blessing and says: "Enough."

Chapter 45

MISTAKES IN THE ORATORY

Should anyone make a mistake in a psalm, responsory, refrain or reading, he must make satisfaction there before all. If he does not use this occasion to humble himself, he will be subjected to more severe punishment for failing to correct by humility the wrong committed through negligence. Children, however, are to be whipped for such a fault.

Chapter 46

FAULTS COMMITTED
IN OTHER MATTERS

If someone commits a fault while at any work—while working in the kitchen, in the storeroom, in serving, in the bakery, in the garden, in any craft or anywhere else—either by breaking or losing something or failing in any other way in any other place, he must at once come before the abbot and community and of his own accord admit his fault and make satisfaction. If it is made known through another, he is to be subjected to more severe correction.

When the cause of the sin lies hidden in his conscience, he is to reveal it only to the abbot or to one of the spiritual elders, who know how to heal their own wounds, as well as those of others, without exposing them and making them public.

Chapter 47

ANNOUNCING THE HOURS
FOR THE WORK OF GOD

It is the abbot's care to announce, day and night, the hour for the Work of God. He may do so personally or delegate the responsibility to a conscientious brother, so that everything may be done at the proper time.

Only those so authorized are to lead psalms and refrains, after the abbot according to their rank. No one should presume to read or sing unless he is able to benefit the hearers; let this be done with humility, seriousness and reverence, and at the abbot's bidding.

Chapter 48

THE DAILY MANUAL LABOR

Idleness is the enemy of the soul. Therefore, the brothers should have specified periods for manual labor as well as for prayerful reading.

We believe that the times for both may be arranged as follows: From Easter to the first of October, they will spend their mornings after Prime till about the fourth hour at whatever work needs to be done. From the fourth hour until the time of Sext, they will devote themselves to reading. But after Sext and their meal, they may rest on their beds in complete silence; should a brother wish to read privately, let him do so, but without disturbing the others. They should say None a little early, about midway through the eighth hour, and then until Vespers they are to return to whatever work is necessary. They must not become distressed if local conditions or their poverty should force them to do the harvesting themselves. When they live by the labor of their hands, as our fathers and the apostles did, then they are really monks. Yet, all things are to be done with moderation on account of the fainthearted.

From the first of October to the beginning of Lent, the brothers ought to devote themselves to reading until the end of the second hour. At this time Terce is said and they are to work at their assigned tasks until None. At the first signal for the hour of None, all put aside their work to be ready for the second signal. Then, after their meal, they will devote themselves to their reading or to the psalms.

During the days of Lent, they should be free in the morning to read until the third hour, after which they will work at their assigned tasks until the end of the tenth hour. During this time of Lent, each one is to receive a book from the library and is to read the whole of it straight through. These books are to be distributed at the beginning of Lent.

Above all, one or two seniors must surely be deputed to make the rounds of the monastery while the brothers are reading. Their duty is to see that no brother is so apathetic as to waste time or engage in idle talk to the neglect of his reading, and so not only harm himself but also distract others. If such a monk is found— God forbid—he should be reproved a first and a second time. If he does not amend, he must be subjected to the punishment of the rule as a warning to others. Further, brothers ought not to associate with one another at inappropriate times.

On Sunday all are to be engaged in reading except those who have been assigned various duties. If anyone is so remiss and indolent that he is unwilling or unable to study or to read, he is to be given some work in order that he may not be idle.

Brothers who are sick or weak should be given a type of work or craft that will keep them busy without overwhelming them or driving them away. The abbot must take their infirmities into account.

Chapter 49

THE OBSERVANCE OF LENT

The life of a monk ought to be a continuous Lent. Since few, however, have the strength for this, we urge the entire community during these days of Lent to keep its manner of life most pure and to wash away in this holy season the negligences of other times. This we can do in a fitting manner by refusing to indulge evil habits and by devoting ourselves to prayer with tears, to reading, compunction of heart and self-denial. During these days, therefore, we will add to the usual measure of our service something by way of private prayer and abstinence from food or drink, so that each of us will have something above the assigned measure to offer God of his own will *with the joy of the Holy Spirit.*[141] In other words, let each one deny himself some food, drink, sleep, needless talking and idle jesting, and look forward to holy Easter with joy and spiritual longing.

Everyone should, however, make known to the abbot what he intends to do, since it ought to be done with his prayer and approval. Whatever is undertaken without the permission of the spiritual father will be reckoned as presumption and vainglory, not deserving a reward. Therefore, everything must be done with the abbot's approval.

Chapter 50

BROTHERS WORKING AT A DISTANCE
OR TRAVELING

Brothers who work so far away that they cannot return to the oratory at the proper time—and the abbot determines that is the case—are to perform the Work of God where they are, and kneel out of reverence for God.

So too, those who have been sent on a journey are not to omit the prescribed hours but to observe them as best they can, not neglecting their measure of service.

Chapter 51

BROTHERS ON A SHORT JOURNEY

If a brother is sent on some errand and expects to return to the monastery that same day, he must not presume to eat outside, even if he receives a pressing invitation, unless perhaps the abbot has ordered it. Should he act otherwise, he will be excommunicated.

Chapter 52

THE ORATORY OF THE MONASTERY

The oratory ought to be what it is called, and nothing else is to be done or stored there. After the Work of God, all should leave in complete silence and with reverence for God, so that a brother who may wish to pray alone will not be disturbed by the insensitivity of another. Moreover, if at other times someone chooses to pray privately, he may simply go in and pray, not in a loud voice, but with tears and heartfelt devotion. Accordingly, anyone who does not pray in this manner is not to remain in the oratory after the Work of God, as we have said; then he will not interfere with anyone else.

Chapter 53

THE RECEPTION OF GUESTS

All guests who present themselves are to be welcomed as Christ, for he himself will say: *I was a stranger and you welcomed me.*[142] Proper honor must be shown *to all, especially to those who share our faith*[143] and to pilgrims.

Once a guest has been announced, the superior and the brothers are to meet him with all the courtesy of love. First of all, they are to pray together and thus be united in peace, but prayer must always precede the kiss of peace because of the delusions of the devil.

All humility should be shown in addressing a guest on arrival or departure. By a bow of the head or by a complete prostration of the body, Christ is to be adored because he is indeed welcomed in them. After the guests have been received, they should be invited to pray; then the superior or an appointed brother will sit with them. The divine law is read to the guest for his instruction, and after that every kindness is shown to him. The superior may break his fast for the sake of a guest, unless it is a day of special fast which cannot be broken. The brothers, however, observe the usual fast. The abbot shall pour water on the hands of the guests, and the abbot with the entire community shall wash their feet. After the washing they will recite this verse: *God, we have received your mercy in the midst of your temple.*[144]

Great care and concern are to be shown in receiving poor

people and pilgrims, because in them more particularly Christ is received; our very awe of the rich guarantees them special respect.

The kitchen for the abbot and guests ought to be separate, so that guests—and monasteries are never without them—need not disturb the brothers when they present themselves at unpredictable hours. Each year, two brothers who can do the work competently are to be assigned to this kitchen. Additional help should be available when needed, so that they can perform this service without grumbling. On the other hand, when the work slackens, they are to go wherever other duties are assigned them. This consideration is not for them alone, but applies to all duties in the monastery; the brothers are to be given help when it is needed, and whenever they are free, they work wherever they are assigned.

The guest quarters are to be entrusted to a God-fearing brother. Adequate bedding should be available there. The house of God should be in the care of wise men who will manage it wisely.

No one is to speak or associate with guests unless he is bidden; however, if a brother meets or sees a guest, he is to greet him humbly, as we have said. He asks for a blessing and continues on his way, explaining that he is not allowed to speak with a guest.

Chapter 54
LETTERS OR GIFTS FOR MONKS

In no circumstances is a monk allowed, unless the abbot says he may, to exchange letters, blessed tokens or small gifts of any kind with his parents or anyone else, or with a fellow monk. He mus not presume to accept gifts sent him even by his parents withou previously telling the abbot. If the abbot orders acceptance, he still has the power to give the gift to whom he will; and the brother for whom it was originally sent must not be distressed, *lest occasion be given to the devil.*[145] Whoever presumes to act otherwise will be subjected to the discipline of the rule.

Chapter 55

THE CLOTHING AND FOOTWEAR
OF THE BROTHERS

The clothing distributed to the brothers should vary according to local conditions and climate, because more is needed in cold regions and less in warmer. This is left to the abbot's discretion. We believe that for each monk a cowl and tunic will suffice in temperate regions; in winter a woolen cowl is necessary, in summer a thinner or worn one; also a scapular for work, and footwear— both sandals and shoes.

Monks must not complain about the color or coarseness of all these articles, but use what is available in the vicinity at a reasonable cost. However, the abbot ought to be concerned about the measurements of these garments that they not be too short but fitted to the wearers.

Whenever new clothing is received, the old should be returned at once and stored in a wardrobe for the poor. To provide for laundering and night wear, every monk will need two cowls and two tunics, but anything more must be taken away as superfluous. When new articles are received, the worn ones—sandals or anything old—must be returned.

Brothers going on a journey should get underclothing from the wardrobe. On their return they are to wash it and give it back. Their cowls and tunics, too, ought to be somewhat better than those they ordinarily wear. Let them get these from the wardrobe before departing, and on returning put them back.

For bedding the monks will need a mat, a woolen blanket and a light covering, as well as a pillow.

The beds are to be inspected frequently by the abbot, lest private possessions be found there. A monk discovered with anything not given him by the abbot must be subjected to very severe punishment. In order that this vice of private ownership may be completely uprooted, the abbot is to provide all things necessary: that is, cowl, tunic, sandals, shoes, belt, knife, stylus, needle, handkerchief and writing tablets. In this way every excuse of lacking some necessity will be taken away.

The abbot, however, must always bear in mind what is said in the Acts of the Apostles: *Distribution was made to each one as he had need.*[146] In this way the abbot will take into account the weaknesses of the needy, not the evil will of the envious; yet in all his judgments he must bear in mind God's retribution.

Chapter 56
THE ABBOT'S TABLE

The abbot's table must always be with guests and travelers. Whenever there are no guests, it is within his right to invite any of the brothers he wishes. However, for the sake of maintaining discipline, one or two seniors must always be left with the brothers.

Chapter 57

THE ARTISANS OF THE MONASTERY

If there are artisans in the monastery, they are to practice their craft with all humility, but only with the abbot's permission. If one of them becomes puffed up by his skillfulness in his craft, and feels that he is conferring something on the monastery, he is to be removed from practicing his craft and not allowed to resume it unless, after manifesting his humility, he is so ordered by the abbot.

Whenever products of these artisans are sold, those responsible for the sale must not dare to practice any fraud. Let them always remember Ananias and Sapphira, who incurred bodily death,[147] lest they and all who perpetrate fraud in monastery affairs suffer spiritual death.

The evil of avarice must have no part in establishing prices, which should, therefore, always be a little lower than people outside the monastery are able to set, *so that in all things God may be glorified.*[148]

Chapter 58

THE PROCEDURE
FOR RECEIVING BROTHERS

Do not grant newcomers to the monastic life an easy entry, but, as the Apostle says, *Test the spirits to see if they are from God.*[149] Therefore, if someone comes and keeps knocking at the door, and if at the end of four or five days he has shown himself patient in bearing his harsh treatment and difficulty of entry, and has persisted in his request, then he should be allowed to enter and stay in the guest quarters for a few days. After that, he should live in the novitiate, where the novices study, eat and sleep.

A senior chosen for his skill in winning souls should be appointed to look after them with careful attention. The concern must be whether the novice truly seeks God and whether he shows eagerness for the Work of God, for obedience and for trials. The novice should be clearly told all the hardships and difficulties that will lead him to God.

If he promises perseverance in his stability, then after two months have elapsed let this rule be read straight through to him, and let him be told: "This is the law under which you are choosing to serve. If you can keep it, come in. If not, feel free to leave." If he still stands firm, he is to be taken back to the novitiate, and again thoroughly tested in patience. After six months have passed, the rule is to be read to him, so that he may know what he is entering. If once more he stands firm, let four months go by, and then read this rule to him again. If after due reflection he promises to observe everything and to obey every command given him, let him then be received into the community. But he must be well aware that, as the law of the rule establishes, from this day he is no longer free to leave the monastery, nor to shake from his neck the yoke of the rule which, in the course of so prolonged a period of reflection, he was free either to reject or to accept.

When he is to be received, he comes before the whole community in the oratory and promises stability, fidelity to monastic life, and obedience. This is done in the presence of God and his saints to impress on the novice that if he ever acts otherwise, he will surely be condemned by the one he mocks. He states his promise in a document drawn up in the name of the saints whose relics are there, and of the abbot, who is present. The novice writes out this document himself, or if he is illiterate, then he asks someone else to write it for him, but himself puts his mark to it and with his own hand lays it on the altar. After he has put it there, the novice himself begins the verse: *Receive me,* Lord, *as you have promised, and I shall live; do not disappoint me in my hope.*[150] The whole community repeats the verse three times, and adds, "Glory be to the Father." Then the novice prostrates himself at the feet of each monk to ask his prayers, and from that very day he is to be counted as one of the community.

If he has any possessions, he should either give them to the poor beforehand, or make a formal donation of them to the monastery, without keeping back a single thing for himself, well aware that from that day he will not have even his own body at his disposal. Then and there in the oratory, he is to be stripped of everything of his own that he is wearing and clothed in what belongs to the monastery. The clothing taken from him is to be put away and kept safely in the wardrobe, so that, should he ever agree to the devil's suggestion and leave the monastery—which God forbid— he can be stripped of the clothing of the monastery before he is cast out. But that document of his which the abbot took from the altar should not be given back to him but kept in the monastery.

Chapter 59

THE OFFERING OF SONS BY NOBLES
OR BY THE POOR

If a member of the nobility offers his son to God in the monastery, and the boy himself is too young, the parents draw up the document mentioned above; then, at the presentation of the gifts, they wrap the document itself and the boy's hand in the altar cloth. That is how they offer him.

As to their property, they either make a sworn promise in this document that they will never personally, never through an intermediary, nor in any way at all, nor at any time, give the boy anything or afford him the opportunity to possess anything; or else, if they are unwilling to do this and still wish to win their reward for making an offering to the monastery, they make a formal donation of the property that they want to give to the monastery, keeping the revenue for themselves, should they so desire. This ought to leave no way open for the boy to entertain any expectations that could deceive and ruin him. May God forbid this, but we have learned from experience that it can happen.

Poor people do the same, but those who have nothing at all simply write the document and, in the presence of witnesses, offer their son with the gifts.

Chapter 60

THE ADMISSION OF PRIESTS
TO THE MONASTERY

If any ordained priest asks to be received into the monastery, do not agree too quickly. However, if he is fully persistent in his request, he must recognize that he will have to observe the full discipline of the rule without any mitigation, knowing that it is written: *Friend, what have you come for?*[151] He should, however, be allowed to stand next to the abbot, to give blessings and to celebrate Mass, provided that the abbot bids him. Otherwise, he must recognize that he is subject to the discipline of the rule, and not make any exceptions for himself, but rather give everyone an example of humility. Whenever there is question of an appointment or of any other business in the monastery, he takes the place that corresponds to the date of his entry into the community, and not that granted him out of respect for his priesthood.

Any clerics who similarly wish to join the community should

be ranked somewhere in the middle, but only if they, too, promise to keep the rule and observe stability.

Chapter 61
THE RECEPTION OF VISITING MONKS

A visiting monk from far away will perhaps present himself and wish to stay as a guest in the monastery. Provided that he is content with the life as he finds it, and does not make excessive demands that upset the monastery, but is simply content with what he finds, he should be received for as long a time as he wishes. He may, indeed, with all humility and love make some reasonable criticisms or observations, which the abbot should prudently consider; it is possible that the Lord guided him to the monastery for this very purpose.

If after a while he wishes to remain and bind himself to stability, he should not be refused this wish, especially as there was time enough, while he was a guest, to judge his character. But if during his stay he has been found excessive in his demands or full of faults, he should certainly not be admitted as a member of the community. Instead, he should be politely told to depart, lest his wretched ways contaminate others.

If, however, he has shown that he is not the kind of man who deserves to be dismissed, let him, on his request, be received as a member of the community. He should even be urged to stay, so that others may learn from his example, because wherever we may be, we are in the service of the same Lord and doing battle for the same King. Further, the abbot may set such a man in a somewhat higher place in the community, if he sees that he deserves it. In fact, whether it is a monk or someone in the priestly or clerical orders mentioned above, the abbot has the power to set any of them above the place that corresponds to the date of his entry, if he sees that his life warrants it.

The abbot must, however, take care never to receive into the community a monk from another known monastery, unless the monk's abbot consents and sends a letter of recommendation, since it is written: *Never do to another what you do not want done to yourself.*[152]

Chapter 62

THE PRIESTS OF THE MONASTERY

Any abbot who asks to have a priest or deacon ordained should choose from his monks one worthy to exercise the priesthood. The monk so ordained must be on guard against conceit or pride, must not presume to do anything except what the abbot commands him, and must recognize that now he will have to subject himself all the more to the discipline of the rule. Just because he is a priest, he may not therefore forget the obedience and discipline of the rule, but must make more and more progress toward God.

He will always take the place that corresponds to the date of his entry into the monastery, except in his duties at the altar, or unless the whole community chooses and the abbot wishes to give him a higher place for the goodness of his life. Yet, he must know how to keep the rule established for deans and priors; should he presume to act otherwise, he must be regarded as a rebel, not as a priest. If after many warnings he does not improve, let the bishop too be brought in as a witness. Should he not amend even then, and his faults become notorious, he is to be dismissed from the monastery, but only if he is so arrogant that he will not submit or obey the rule.

Chapter 63

COMMUNITY RANK

The monks keep their rank in the monastery according to the date of their entry, the virtue of their lives, and the decision of the abbot. The abbot is not to disturb the flock entrusted to him nor make any unjust arrangements, as though he had the power to do whatever he wished. He must constantly reflect that he will have to give God an account of all his decisions and actions. Therefore, when the monks come for the kiss of peace and for Communion, when they lead psalms or stand in choir, they do so in the order decided by the abbot or already existing among them. Absolutely nowhere shall age automatically determine rank. Remember that Samuel and Daniel were still boys when they judged their elders.[153] Therefore, apart from those mentioned above whom the abbot has for some overriding consideration promoted, or for a specific reason demoted, all the rest should keep to the order of their entry. For example, someone who came to the monastery at the second hour of the day must recognize that he is junior to someone who came at the first hour, regardless of age or distinction. Boys, however, are to be disciplined in everything by everyone.

The younger monks, then, must respect their seniors, and the seniors must love their juniors. When they address one another, no one should be allowed to do so simply by name; rather, the seniors call the younger monks "brother" and the younger monks call their seniors *nonnus,* which is translated as "venerable father." But the abbot, because we believe that he holds the place of Christ, is to be called "lord" and "abbot," not for any claim of his own, but out of honor and love for Christ. He, for his part, must reflect on this, and in his behavior show himself worthy of such honor.

Wherever brothers meet, the junior asks his senior for a blessing. When an older monk comes by, the younger rises and offers him a seat, and does not presume to sit down unless the older bids him. In this way, they do what the words of Scripture say: *They should each try to be the first to show respect to the other.*[154]

In the oratory and at table, small boys and youths are kept in rank and under discipline. Outside or anywhere else, they should be supervised and controlled until they are old enough to be responsible.

Chapter 64

THE ELECTION OF AN ABBOT

In choosing an abbot, the guiding principle should always be that the man placed in office be the one selected either by the whole community acting unanimously in the fear of God, or by some part of the community, no matter how small, which possesses sounder judgment. Goodness of life and wisdom in teaching must be the criteria for choosing the one to be made abbot, even if he is the last in community rank.

May God forbid that a whole community should conspire to elect a man who goes along with its own evil ways. But if it does, and if the bishop of the diocese or the abbots or Christians in the area come to know of these evil ways to any extent, they must block the success of this wicked conspiracy, and set a worthy steward in charge of God's house. They may be sure that they will receive a generous reward for this, if they do it with pure motives and zeal for God's honor. Conversely, they may be equally sure that to neglect to do so is sinful.

Once in office, the abbot must keep constantly in mind the nature of the burden he has received, and remember to whom he will have *to give an account of his stewardship.*[155] Let him recognize that his goal must be profit for the monks, not preeminence for himself. He ought, therefore, to be learned in divine law, so that he has a treasury of knowledge from which he can *bring out what is new and what is old.*[156] He must be chaste, temperate and merciful. He should always *let mercy triumph over judgment*[157] so that he too may win mercy. He must hate faults but love the brothers. When he must punish them, he should use prudence and avoid extremes; otherwise, by rubbing too hard to remove the rust, he may break the vessel. He is to distrust his own frailty and remember *not to crush the bruised reed.*[158] By this we do not mean that he should allow faults to flourish, but rather, as we have already said, he should prune them away with prudence and love as he sees best for each individual. Let him strive to be loved rather than feared.

Excitable, anxious, extreme, obstinate, jealous or oversuspicious he must not be. Such a man is never at rest. Instead, he must show forethought and consideration in his orders, and whether the task he assigns concerns God or the world, he should be discerning and moderate, bearing in mind the discretion of holy Jacob, who said: *If I drive my flocks too hard, they will all die in a single day.*[159] Therefore, drawing on this and other examples of discretion, the mother of virtues, he must so arrange everything that the strong have something to yearn for and the weak nothing to run from.

He must, above all, keep this rule in every particular, so that when he has ministered well he will hear from the Lord what that good servant heard who gave his fellow servants grain at the proper time: *I tell you solemnly,* he said, *he sets him over all his possessions.*[160]

Chapter 65

THE PRIOR OF THE MONASTERY

Too often in the past, the appointment of a prior has been the source of serious contention in monasteries. Some priors, puffed up by the evil spirit of pride and thinking of themselves as second abbots, usurp tyrannical power and foster contention and discord in their communities. This occurs especially in monasteries where the same bishop and the same abbots appoint both abbot and prior. It is easy to see what an absurd arrangement this is, because from the very first moment of his appointment as prior he is given grounds for pride, as his thoughts suggest to him that he is exempt from his abbot's authority. "After all, you were made prior by the same men who made the abbot."

This is an open invitation to envy, quarrels, slander, rivalry, factions and disorders of every kind, with the result that, while abbot and prior pursue conflicting policies, their own souls are inevitably endangered by this discord; and at the same time the monks under them take sides and so go to their ruin. The responsibility for this evil and dangerous situation rests on the heads of those who initiated such a state of confusion.

For the preservation of peace and love we have, therefore, judged it best for the abbot to make all decisions in the conduct of his monastery. If possible, as we have already established, the whole operation of the monastery should be managed through deans under the abbot's direction. Then, so long as it is entrusted to more than one, no individual will yield to pride. But if local conditions call for it, or the community makes a reasonable and humble request, and the abbot judges it best, then let him, with the advice of God-fearing brothers, choose the man he wants and himself make him his prior. The prior for his part is to carry out respectfully what his abbot assigns to him, and do nothing contrary to the abbot's wishes or arrangements, because the more he is set above the rest, the more he should be concerned to keep what the rule commands.

If this prior is found to have serious faults, or is led astray by conceit and grows proud, or shows open contempt for the holy rule, he is to be warned verbally as many as four times. If he does not amend, he is to be punished as required by the discipline of the rule. Then, if he still does not reform, he is to be deposed from the rank of prior and replaced by someone worthy. If after all that, he is not a peaceful and obedient member of the community, he should even be expelled from the monastery. Yet the abbot should reflect that he must give God an account of all his judgments, lest the flames of jealousy or rivalry sear his soul.

Chapter 66
THE PORTER OF THE MONASTERY

At the door of the monastery, place a sensible old man who knows how to take a message and deliver a reply, and whose age keeps him from roaming about. This porter will need a room near the entrance so that visitors will always find him there to answer them. As soon as anyone knocks, or a poor man calls out, he replies, "Thanks be to God" or "Your blessing, please"; then, with all the gentleness that comes from the fear of God, he provides a prompt answer with the warmth of love. Let the porter be given one of the younger brothers if he needs help.

The monastery should, if possible, be so constructed that within it all necessities, such as water, mill and garden are contained, and the various crafts are practiced. Then there will be no need for the monks to roam outside, because this is not at all good for their souls.

We wish this rule to be read often in the community, so that none of the brothers can offer the excuse of ignorance.

Chapter 67

BROTHERS SENT ON A JOURNEY

Brothers sent on a journey will ask the abbot and community to pray for them. All absent brothers should always be remembered at the closing prayer of the Work of God. When they come back from a journey, they should, on the very day of their return, lie face down on the floor of the oratory at the conclusion of each of the customary hours of the Work of God. They ask the prayers of all for their faults, in case they may have been caught off guard on the way by seeing some evil thing or hearing some idle talk.

No one should presume to relate to anyone else what he saw or heard outside the monastery, because that causes the greatest harm. If anyone does so presume, he shall be subjected to the punishment of the rule. So too shall anyone who presumes to leave the enclosure of the monastery, or go anywhere, or do anything at all, however small, without the abbot's order.

Chapter 68

ASSIGNMENT OF IMPOSSIBLE TASKS
TO A BROTHER

A brother may be assigned a burdensome task or something he cannot do. If so, he should, with complete gentleness and obedience, accept the order given him. Should he see, however, that the weight of the burden is altogether too much for his strength, then he should choose the appropriate moment and explain patiently to his superior the reasons why he cannot perform the task. This he ought to do without pride, obstinacy or refusal. If after the explanation the superior is still determined to hold to his original order, then the junior must recognize that this is best for him. Trusting in God's help, he must in love obey.

Chapter 69

THE PRESUMPTION OF DEFENDING
ANOTHER IN THE MONASTERY

Every precaution must be taken that one monk does not presume in any circumstance to defend another in the monastery or to be his champion, even if they are related by the closest ties of blood. In no way whatsoever shall the monks presume to do this, because it can be a most serious source and occasion of contention. Anyone who breaks this rule is to be sharply restrained.

Chapter 70

THE PRESUMPTION OF STRIKING
ANOTHER MONK AT WILL

In the monastery every occasion for presumption is to be avoided, and so we decree that no one has the authority to excommunicate or strike any of his brothers unless he has been given this power by the abbot. *Those who sin should be reprimanded in the presence of all, that the rest may fear.*[161] Boys up to the age of fifteen should, however, be carefully controlled and supervised by everyone, provided that this too is done with moderation and common sense. If a brother, without the abbot's command, assumes any power over those older or, even in regard to boys, flares up and treats them unreasonably, he is to be subjected to the discipline of the rule. After all, it is written: *Never do to another what you do not want done to yourself.*[162]

Chapter 71
MUTUAL OBEDIENCE

Obedience is a blessing to be shown by all, not only to the abbot but also to one another as brothers, since we know that it is by this way of obedience that we go to God. Therefore, although orders of the abbot or of the priors appointed by him take precedence, and no unofficial order may supersede them, in every other instance younger monks should obey their seniors with all love and concern. Anyone found objecting to this should be reproved.

If a monk is reproved in any way by his abbot or by one of his seniors, even for some very small matter, or if he gets the impression that one of his seniors is angry or disturbed with him, however slightly, he must, then and there without delay, cast himself on the ground at the other's feet to make satisfaction, and lie there until the disturbance is calmed by a blessing. Anyone who refuses to do this should be subjected to corporal punishment or, if he is stubborn, should be expelled from the monastery.

Chapter 72

THE GOOD ZEAL OF MONKS

Just as there is a wicked zeal of bitterness which separates from God and leads to hell, so there is a good zeal which separates from evil and leads to God and everlasting life. This, then, is the good zeal which monks must foster with fervent love: *They should each try to be the first to show respect to the other,*[163] supporting with the greatest patience one another's weaknesses of body or behavior, and earnestly competing in obedience to one another. No one is to pursue what he judges better for himself, but instead, what he judges better for someone else. To their fellow monks they show the pure love of brothers; to God, loving fear; to their abbot, unfeigned and humble love. Let them prefer nothing whatever to Christ, and may he bring us all together to everlasting life.

Chapter 73

THIS RULE ONLY A BEGINNING
OF PERFECTION

The reason we have written this rule is that, by observing it in monasteries, we can show that we have some degree of virtue and the beginnings of monastic life. But for anyone hastening on to the perfection of monastic life, there are the teachings of the holy Fathers, the observance of which will lead him to the very heights of perfection. What page, what passage of the inspired books of the Old and New Testaments is not the truest of guides for human life? What book of the holy catholic Fathers does not resoundingly summon us along the true way to reach the Creator? Then, besides the *Conferences* of the Fathers, their *Institutes* and their *Lives,* there is also the rule of our holy father Basil. For observant and obedient monks, all these are nothing less than tools for the cultivation of virtues; but as for us, they make us blush for shame at being so slothful, so unobservant, so negligent. Are you hastening toward your heavenly home? Then with Christ's help, keep this little rule that we have written for beginners. After that, you can set out for the loftier summits of the teaching and virtues we mentioned above, and under God's protection you will reach them. Amen.

1. Rom 13:11.
2. Ps 94 (95):8.
3. Rev 2:7.
4. Ps 33(34):12.
5. John 12:35.
6. Ps 33(34):13.
7. Ps 33(34):14–15.
8. Isa 58:9.
9. 1 Thess 2:12.
10. Ps 14(15):1.
11. Ps 14(15):2-3.
12. Ps 14(15):4; 136(137):9.
13. Ps 14(15):4.
14. Ps 113(115:1):9.
15. 1 Cor 15:10.
16. 2 Cor 10:17.
17. Matt 7:24–25.
18. Rom 2:4.
19. Ezek 33:11.
20. Prov 27:21.
21. Rom 8:15.
22. Ps 39(40):11.
23. Isa 1:2; Ezek 20:27.
24. 1 Cor 9:27.
25. Ps 49(50):16–17.
26. Matt 7:3.
27. Gal 3:28; Eph 6:8.
28. Rom 2:11.
29. 2 Tim 4:2.
30. 1 Sam 2:11–4:18.
31. Prov 29:19.
32. Prov 23:14.
33. Matt 6:33.
34. Ps 33(34):10.
35. Sir 32:24.
36. Matt 22:37–39; Mark 12:30–31; Luke 10:27.
37. Rom 13:9.
38. Matt 19:18; MARK 10:19; LUKE 18:20.
39. 1 PET 2:17.
40. Tob 4:16; Matt 7:12; LUKE 6:31.
41. Matt 16:24; Luke 9:23.
42. 1 Cor 9:27.
43. Matt 25:36.
44. 1 Thess 5:15; 1Pet 3:9.
45. Matt 5:44; Luke 6:27.
46. Matt 5:10.
47. Titus 1:7; 1Tim 3:3.
48. Rom 12:11.
49. Gal 5:16.

50. Matt 23:3.
51. 1 Cor 2:9.
52. Ps 17(18):45.
53. Luke 10:16.
54. Matt 7:14.
55. John 6:38.
56. Luke 10:16.
57. 2 Cor 9:7.
58. Ps 38(39):2–3.
59. Prov 10:19.
60. Prov 18:21.
61. Luke 14:11; 18:14.
62. Ps 130(131):1.
63. Ps 130(131):2.
64. Gen 28:12.
65. Ps 35(36):2.
66. Ps 7:10.
67. Ps 93(94):11.
68. Ps 138(139):2.
69. Ps 75(76):11.
70. Ps 17(18):24.
71. Sir 18:30.
72. Matt 6:10.
73. Prov 16:25.
74. Ps 13(14):1.
75. Ps 37(38):10.
76. Sir 18:30.
77. Prov 15:3.
78. Ps 13(14):2.
79. Ps 13(14):3.
80. Ps 49(50):21.
81. John 6:38.

82. Phil 2:8.
83. Matt 10:22.
84. Ps 26(27):14.
85. Rom 8:36; Ps 43(44):22.
86. Rom 8:37.
87. Ps 65(66):10–11.
88. Ps 65(66):12.
89. Matt 5:39–41.
90. 2 Cor 11:26; 1Cor 4:12.
91. Ps 36(37):5.
92. Ps 105(106):1; Ps
    117(118):1.
93. Ps 31(32):5.
94. Ps 72(73):22–23.
95. Ps 21(22):7.
96. Ps 87(88):16.
97. Ps 118(119):71, 73.
98. Prov 10:19.
99. Ps 139(140):12.
100. Sir 21:20.
101. Luke 18:13.
102. Ps 37(38):7–9; Ps
    118(119):107.
103. 1 John 4:18.
104. Ps 50(51):17.
105. Matt 6:12.
106. Matt 6:13.
107. Ps 118(119):164.
108. Ps 118(119):164.
109. Ps 118(119):62.
110. Ps 118(119):164,62.
111. Ps 69(70):2.

112. Ps 69(70):2.
113. Prov 15:3.
114. Ps 2:11.
115. Ps 46(47):8.
116. Ps 137(138):1.
117. Matt 18:15–16.
118. 1 Cor 5:5.
119. Matt 9:12.
120. 2 Cor 2:7.
121. 2 Cor 2:8.
122. Ezek 34:3–4.
123. Luke 15:5.
124. 1 Cor 5:13.
125. 1 Cor 7:15.
126. 1 Tim 3:13.
127. Sir 18:16.
128. Matt 18:6.
129. Acts 4:32.
130. Acts 4:35.
131. Dan 3:52; Ps 85(86):17.
132. Ps 69(70):2.
133. Matt 25:36.
134. Matt 25:40.
135. Ps 50(51):17.
136. Eph 4:27; 1 Tim 5:14.
137. Luke 21:34.

138. 1 Cor 7:7.
139. Sir 19:2.
140. Eph 4:27; 1 Tim 5:14.
141. 1 Thess 1:6.
142. Matt 25:35.
143. Gal 6:10.
144. Ps 47(48):10.
145. Eph 4:27; 1 Tim 5:14.
146. Acts 4:35.
147. Acts 5:1–11.
148. 1 Pet 4:11.
149. 1 John 4:1.
150. Ps 118(119):116.
151. Matt 26:50.
152. Tob 4:16.
153. 1 Sam 3; Dan 13:44–62.
154. Rom 12:10.
155. Luke 16:2.
156. Matt 13:52.
157. Jas 2:13.
158. Isa 42:3.
159. Gen 33:13.
160. Matt 24:47.
161. 1 Tim 5:20.
162. Tob 4:16.
163. Rom 12:10.

SUGGESTIONS
FOR FURTHER READING

BROOKE, CHRISTOPHER. *The Monastic World.* New York, 1974.

CHADWICK, O. *Western Asceticism.* London, 1958.

CHITTY, D.J. *The Desert a City.* Oxford, 1966.

FRY, TIMOTHY. *RB 1980: The Rule of St. Benedict in Latin and English with Notes.* Collegeville, Minn., 1981

HILPISCH, S. *Benedictinism Through Changing Centuries.* Collegeville, Minn., 1958.

KNOWLES, DAVID. *Christian Monasticism.* London, 1969.

——— *From Pachomius to Ignatius.* Oxford, 1966.

LECKEY, DOLORES. *The Ordinary Way: A Family Spirituality* New York: Crossroad, 1982.

LECLERCQ, O.S.B., JEAN. *The Love of Learning and the Desir for God.* New York: Fordham University Press, 1985.

LECLERCQ, O.S.B., JEAN, FRANCOIS VANDENBROUCKE AN LOUIS BOUYER. *A History of Christian Spirituality,* Vol. I *The Spirituality of the Middle Ages.* Minneapolis, Minn Seabury Press, 1968.

McCANN, J. *St. Benedict.* London, 1939.

PARRY, O.S.B., DAVID. *Households of God*. London: Darton, Longman and Todd, 1980.

WAAL, ESTHER DE. *Seeking God: The Way of St. Benedict*. London: Fount Paperbacks, 1985.

ZARNECKI, GEORGE. *The Monastic Achievement*. New York, 1972.

TIMOTHY FRY, the editor of *The Rule of St. Benedict in English*, has been a monk of St. Benedict's Abbey in Atchison, Kansas, since professing his vows in 1936. Ordained a priest in 1941, he received a Ph.D. in English from the University of North Carolina in 1948. He then taught at St. Benedict's College in Kansas until becoming editor, from 1968 through 1982, of the *American Benedictine Review*. From 1975 to its publication in 1981 he headed a team of eighteen Benedictine monks and nuns to produce a new American edition of the Rule of St. Benedict, the text of this book.

THOMAS MOORE (1940–   ) lived a monastic life for twelve years as member of the Servite Order, leaving before being ordained a priest. After receiving a Ph.D. from Syracuse University and years of college teaching, he began a private psychotherapy practice. Since 1985 he has lived in New England and is the author of, among other books, the bestselling *Care of the Soul* (1992), *Soul Mates* (1994), and *The Re–Enchantment of Everyday Life* (1996).

JOHN F. THORNTON is a literary agent, former book editor, and the coeditor, with Katharine Washburn, of *Dumbing Down* (1996) and *Tongues of Angels, Tongues of Men: A Book of Sermons* (forthcoming, 1998). He lives in New York City.

SUSAN B. VARENNE is a New York City high-school teacher with a strong avocational interest in and wide experience of spiritual literature (MA, The University of Chicago Divinity School; Ph.D., Columbia University).